GUIDING
·····················
STARS

GUIDING
STARS

A selection of writings, recollections and images
chosen to convey some of the joys and anxieties,
achievements and disappointments
experienced by the generations of people who have
either used guide dogs or helped to provide them.

Compiled and edited by
Peter Ireson

Lennard Publishing

First published in 1993 by
Lennard Publishing
a division of Lennard Associates Ltd
Mackerye End
Harpenden
Herts AL5 5DR

ISBN 1 85291 109 3

British Library Cataloguing in Publication Data
is available

The publishers and the editor are grateful for the permission
of *Punch* to reproduce the cartoons on pages 25, 35, 41,
53, 59, 95, 103, 108, 114,136 and to the
Herts Advertiser for the photograph on page 46.

Cover photograph:
Joe Errington with his former guide dog, Gundo.

Printed and bound in Great Britain by
The Bath Press

CONTENTS

FOREWORD
BY DAVID BLUNKETT, MP

Like every good anthology, this one has laughter and sadness, has pathos and insights sufficient for all. Dipping into the experiences of men and women down through the century is an insight not only into the work of guide dogs but into the changing pattern of social behaviour, of attitudes and expectations.

Like David Scott-Blackhall, who became a familiar voice on Radio 4's *In Touch* programme, I myself shied away from having a guide dog for several years because of what he describes as the "sentimentality" with which some guide dog owners treat their animals. Like him, I came to understand the value of the three dogs which I have so far owned and which have brought me the gift which every guide dog owner knows to be the most valuable of all – independence.

The testament given by many contributors serves as an ample reminder of the way in which, since the first German Shepherds were trained during the First World War, guide dogs have made their contribution to providing freedom for blind men and women to take their place as equal and full citizens in modern society. Independence and dignity are seldom valued until they are lost, so for blind people, whose mobility is so crucial to a normal social and work life, a guide dog can literally be a passport to success.

There are, of course, those who do not like dogs and for whom a guide dog would be entirely the wrong form of mobility aid. A dog is a dog. It requires love and care and attention – taking out in driving rain and grooming when it is covered in mud – just as much as it needs discipline. There are still many people, including some guide dog owners, who think that they are dealing with a pet, or in some sad cases a substitute for human friendship. A guide dog is a friend and companion, but its foremost task is to act as an aid to mobility, and to perform this job it needs to be alert at work, on duty and whenever it is in harness.

There are of course those, as some of the tales told illustrate, who resent guide dogs and the independence they bring. Probably one of the most sad extracts in the anthology is the letter to "Archibald" by a woman seeking a dependent husband rather than an independent and equal loved one. There are other extracts such as the recollections of the independence by Alfred Morgan on Merseyside, which illustrate the freedom which owner and dog can achieve when working together at their best.

As someone who travels the length and breadth of Britain and has taken internal flights with my dog on more than one occasion, I have marvelled at some of the experiences related in the anthology. Many of the feelings expressed by guide dog owners down through the decades, I have shared. The exhilaration of working with my dog at the peak of its abilities, through the busy pedestrian and vehicle traffic of London or on the underground with people crowded in like cattle; and the sadness and sense of loss at the death of my dog after years of faithful service.

My first dog, Ruby, was a pedigree Golden Labrador and a dog of character. At the age of 10 she had had enough of working and decided to let me know. She devised a limp. Staggering along with a very good imitation of bad arthritis inevitably meant that The Guide Dogs for the Blind Association recommended retirement. Imagine our surprise when as soon as the harness was no longer to be put over her head – which had evoked a rush behind the television in the last few months of her working life – she suddenly managed to shake off the limp altogether. The stories about her behaviour (or rather her misbehaviour) then poured out. Ruby had always been more a mischievous and lovable scavenger, than an exemplary guide dog. This was partly my own fault in the early days for not practising what I preached in terms of discipline, and partly an irrepressible nature which made it very difficult to be angry with her.

My second dog, Teddy, was probably the most famous dog in Britain. He was a Curly Coat Retriever-Labrador cross and a giant of a dog. He soon became a familiar sight on BBC TV's *Question Time* – sleeping through the boring questions – and was the first dog ever to be allowed in the Chamber of the House of Commons when I was elected to Parliament in June 1987. Sadly, a year later, at the remarkable age of 12, he was taken ill and six weeks later he was dead. I do not mind admitting the grief and loss which I felt and which is mirrored on a numer of occasions in the feeling displayed in recollections throughout this book.

Each dog is an individual and works differently. At their best, owner and dog complement each other's strengths, but it is a partnership and both have a part to play.

My third dog, Offa, a German Shepherd-Golden Retriever first-time cross, excels in dificult circumstances where there is a real challenge whilst, on occasions, allowing his natural exuberance to override his training. It is this very exuberance which has pulled him through. In the Autumn of 1991 he was scared by fireworks a couple of weeks before bonfire night and took off over the garden fence and under a van. After six weeks he began to pull round and slowly recovered his health and strength. Tragically (during the 1992 General Election) Offa was taken desperately ill in the middle of one night when I was staying in a Bristol hotel as part of my General Election schedule around the country. Fortunately, I was able to get him to an all-night vet, who diagnosed stomach torsions, and the following morning, after a two and a half hour operation, I went to visit him. Despite the tubes and wires that were keeping him going, and the anaesthetic which was keeping him sedated, there was just the slightest thump of his tail on the floor as he tried to raise his head – the vet pronounced that against all the odds he thought he would pull through! Ten days later I had him back home and, despite having half his stomach removed and a prognosis that he would never work again, he bounced back to full health and a place at the despatch box in the House of Commons.

Each guide dog owner has a tale to tell about the amusing times. In my case, they include the sherry trifles that disappeared without so much as a flick of the head, when my first dog Ruby was passing a sweet trolley of goodies. Or Teddy, who used to carry the trunk of a tree in his mouth and who one day separated two elderly ladies walking in front of me, by attempting to run between them, stick in mouth. They were relieved indeed to find that it was only a big woolly brown dog!

There can also be embarrassment, and the need to laugh at yourself, when your dignity is punctured. I remember one day when I was walking in the woods. I called Offa (who is extremely good on recall) and wondered after a couple of minutes where he had got to. Two walkers coming towards me enquired whether I had two dogs. "No, just the one," I replied, "but I have lost him." "Oh it's alright," they said, "he's been sitting beside you for the past few minutes." As the rascal normally would have nudged my hand, he had obviously decided to see how long it would take before I realised that he was there!

My thanks, like those of guide dog owners down through this century, go to the men and women who have puppy-walked, trained, cared-for and raised funds to provide the guide dogs which have brought both pleasure and increased opportunity to so many people. I commend the anthology, and thank Peter Ireson for the time and care he has taken in compiling it.

* *

✯ Chapter One ✯

THE PIONEER SPIRIT

The main theme of this book is the joy that guide dogs have brought to the lives of thousands of blind people. Nowadays, this partnership between man and dog is taken for granted, and the sight of a Labrador or golden retriever leading its owner swiftly and skilfully through the crowds excites little curiosity. Admiration, perhaps, but certainly not surprise.

It was not always so, of course. Working dogs, other than sheep dogs, were virtually unknown in Britain in the early years of this century and the idea of using them to guide blind people was not received everywhere with enthusiasm. It is worth setting the scene for the guide dog owners whose tales fill most of the following pages by looking back briefly to those pioneering days.

The modern guide dog movement was launched by the German Red Cross Ambulance Dogs Association, which employed dogs during the First World War to locate battlefield casualties. Acting on the suggestion of a Viennese doctor, they decided to start training some of their dogs to lead men blinded in the fighting, and their first guide dog was handed over to a blind veteran, Paul Feyen, in October 1916.

From then on the work developed rapidly. A school that could train 600 dogs and their blind owners every year was established at Oldenburg and classes for blind civilians were added to the veterans' programme in 1922. Another school was opened by the German Shepherd Dog Association at Potsdam in 1923, after which progress was so rapid that by the early 1930s there were over 4,000 guide dogs in Germany.

In Britain, however, the idea of dogs leading blind people was received with some scepticism.

Early Doubts

From Victory over Blindness, *published in 1919, by Sir Arthur Pearson, the founder of St. Dunstan's.*

In the early part of 1918 I read an account of arrangements that were being made in France for the special training of dogs to be used as guides for blinded soldiers. Very interesting particulars were afforded of the special training given to these dogs with the object of teaching them to keep exactly in front of the man whom they were taking along, to give him warning of steps, to keep him from hitting against obstacles and to note the approach of motors and other vehicles. As I read the article it seemed to me that it would need a very special brand of dog intelligence if the canine guide were to be brought up to the point that would make him really trustworthy. Besides this, I had a feeling – which I had no doubt the men of St. Dunstan's fully shared with me – that a dog at the end of a string was apt to remind one a little too much of the blind beggar with his tapping stick and shuffling gait. However, I sent over to France for further

Woodcut from 'The Blind Beggar of Bethnal Green', 1750

particulars, but was not surprised to receive a reply telling me that the idea had not proved as practical as was expected and had been abandoned.

The Potsdam Experience

Outside of Germany there was little or no interest in guide dogs until an enterprising American, Mrs. Dorothy Harrison Eustis, came on the scene. Mrs. Eustis lived in Switzerland, where she trained dogs for police, military and customs work, and during a visit to Germany in 1927 she was taken to the Potsdam guide dog school. Her enthusiasm for what she saw there was so great that she wrote an article about the German guide dog programme for the American magazine Saturday Evening Post *which was published on 5 November 1927. She described the training of the dogs and the blind students, and then went on to tell of her wonder and amazement when she first saw one of the men set off with his guide for a walk.*

I shall never forget the change that came over one man as he turned away from that gate. It was as though a complete trans-formation had taken place before my eyes. One moment it was an uncertain, shuffling blind man, tapping with a cane, the next it was an assured person, with his dog firmly in hand and his head up, who walked toward us quickly and firmly, giving his orders in a low, confident voice. That one quick glimpse of the crying need for guidance and companionship in the lonely, all-enveloping darkness stood out clearly before my swimming eyes ...

I quickly asked permission to follow him on his walk, first getting a few details about him. He had never before owned a dog, and since his blindness had been led everywhere by a member of his family; on arriving at the school he had been particularly nervous, helpless and lacking in confidence. He was a man of about forty-five, thick-set and husky, who had evidently been accustomed to lots of exercise and had become overfat through lack of it. He passed us whistling through his teeth and feeling for a cigarette, his dog looking us over with an appraising eye. I turned quietly and followed. Walking at a good pace, the pair went down the street to the first crossing, where the dog pulled back to indicate the curb. The man's cigarette was apparently his last, as he gave orders to be led to the tobacco shop, went in, made his purchases and then continued his walk.

The walk lay through the crowded shopping street with all the traffic of a big city, its noises and distractions, its scents and stray dogs on mischief or business bent. Understanding, responsibility and never failing protection radiated from that blind leader as he went about his work. His attitude was, "You mind your business and I'll mind mine," as he threaded his way along the street, and the pair went much more quickly without interference than I, who continually bumped into people in my efforts to keep up. I was amazed at the pace; I had started

by walking briskly, but found the distance ever widening between us and the need to make it up every so often on a jog trot.

The streets in German cities are wide and in many places lined with two or three rows of trees and paths. To keep cyclists from riding along these paths barriers have been put up at intervals with narrow openings for pedestrians. The barriers are of one bar each and about the height of a man's waist. I had been told at the school that one of the hardest things to teach a dog was to pass between these barriers and not under them, the way being clear for the dog but not for the man, who would receive the full force of the bar across his middle without warning, so I was interested to follow the pair into one of these wide, shady lanes on the homeward leg.

A couple strolling ahead had dropped a coat directly in the path, but man and dog skirted it and the dog immediately came back to a line that would lead him between the barriers, although for him it would have been simpler and shorter to go under. There was a big catch in my throat as I saw them turn into the school grounds, together with other pairs coming from different directions, and I knew that I was converted. It had not been a particular exhibition staged for my special benefit, but just one of the many dogs turned out every month with his blind master. There were no fireworks, no display, no excuses, no muddling, but honest work done by honest dogs, and my hat was off to those who had worked out and perfected such a method of sympathetic training.

The Seeing Eye

Mrs. Eustis's article drew responses from a number of blind Americans, but it was one from a young insurance salesman, Morris Frank, that persuaded her to start guide dog training herself. With help from Germany, a dog was trained at Mrs. Eustis's kennels in Switzerland and Frank went over to learn how to use it in April 1928. He travelled back to the United States in June on the liner Tuscania *and met his first real challenge when one of the crowd of reporters who met the ship in New York dared him to cross West Street. He described the experience in* First Lady of the Seeing Eye, *published in 1957.*

We entered a street so noisy it was almost like entering a wall of sound. She went about four paces and halted. A deafening roar and a rush of hot air told me a tremendous truck was swooshing past so near that Buddy could have lifted her nose and touched it. She moved forward again into the ear-splitting clangor, stopped, backed up and started again. I lost all sense of direction and surrendered myself entirely to the dog. I shall never forget the next three minutes. Ten-ton trucks rocketing past, cabs blowing

The trio that launched the guide dog movement outside Germany in the late 1920s: Mrs Dorothy Eustis, the owner of a training school in Switzerland for police and army dogs who saw what was being done in Germany and wrote an enthusiastic article about the work in America's Saturday Evening Post; *Morris Frank, the blind salesman who was told about the article and asked Mrs Eustis to train a guide dog for him and to help him set up a training school in the United States; and Buddy, the guide dog that was trained in Switzerland for Frank in 1928.*

their horns in our ears, drivers shouting at us. One fellow yelled, "You damned fool, do you want to get killed?"

When we finally got to the other side and I realized what a really magnificent job she had done, I leaned over and gave Buddy a great big hug and told her what a good, good girl she was. "She sure is a good girl," exclaimed a voice at my elbow – one of the photographers. "I had to come over in a cab, and some of the fellows who tried to cross with you are still back on the other side!"

Soon after Frank's return to the United States, he and Mrs. Eustis founded The Seeing Eye to provide guide dogs for more American blind people. Back in Switzerland, Mrs. Eustis then established a school, which she called L'Oeil qui Voit after the American venture, in order to train instructors and trial dogs for other countries wishing to establish guide dog training programmes.

Greatly Influenced

At the end of 1929, Captain Ian Fraser, who had succeeded Sir Arthur Pearson as head of St. Dunstan's, visited L'Oeil qui Voit and a guide dog school in Berlin. He returned "greatly influenced in favour" of the guide dog by what he had heard and experienced and thought that an experiment should be tried in England. However he recognised a possible obstacle to success, as he confessed in this passage from an article in the St. Dunstan's Review *of February 1930.*

There is one factor which is unknown at present and in regard to which continental experience gives us no clue – namely, the attitude of the English blinded soldier towards the proposition that he should have a dog guide. He may not receive the idea with an open unprejudiced mind. The desire to disassociate himself in his independent outlook upon life, from the traditional idea of a blind man and his dog, may be very strong. I should have taken this view myself soon after I was blinded, for I can well remember the immense trouble I would take in those early days to try to avoid people noticing that I could not see. This was, I think, partly the desire to behave as normally as possible, and partly a measure of self-defence against the awkwardness caused by the excessive sentimentality of a few of the people whom one used to meet. The passage of time, however, alters one's attitude in these matters a little – at least it has altered mine – and I have long ago become accustomed to the fact that I am blind. While I may still strive to do things normally it does not upset me to be recognised as a blinded soldier, as it used to do. I think perhaps this change of attitude may have been experienced by many of my comrades throughout the country, and now that they have become known and respected in the neighbourhoods in which they live, there will perhaps not be the same objection in their minds to the association with the dog as might have been the case earlier. I picture the blinded soldier walking, upright and confident, with his dog by his side, and his friends who meet him being interested and full of admiration for his and the animal's skill in getting over their very great difficulties.

[Despite Captain Fraser's enthusiasm for guide dogs, the Council of St. Dunstan's was not convinced that the arguments in favour of them were strong enough to justify the launch of a training programme. It was not long, however, before others took up the cause.]

The Newspaper Appeal

A few weeks after Captain Fraser's article appeared in the St. Dunstan's Review, *The Times published an article by Fraser about the possibility of introducing guide dogs in Britain. A short piece in the* Liverpool Echo *on 10 April also referred to the possibility. On 21 April the* Echo *published a letter from Robert Tissyman, a local politician, asking dog lovers who wished to help blind people to offer their services to the Liverpool branch of the National Institute for the Blind. Tissyman's appeal produced only one response, a letter from Miss Muriel Crooke, who lived across the Mersey in Wallasey and was secretary of the local Alsatian League.*

A short time later she went to meet Musgrave Frankland, who ran the NIB's Liverpool branch, and came away determined to explore further. She got in touch with Captain Alan Sington, a breeder and trainer of Alsatians – as German shepherd dogs were then called in Britain. Sington had been in Germany with Lady Kitty Ritson and other British breeders in September 1928 when Lady Kitty was given a former guide dog called Lona, and he had probably told Miss Crooke of the gift. He replied to Miss Crooke on 5 May 1930.

Dear Miss Crooke,

I saw Captain Fraser a few days ago and I fear that, for the present at any rate, the matter has been dropped by St. Dunstan's partly because if they provide one man with a dog they will have to provide all their people with dogs. To provide and train a thousand dogs, etc., etc., would cost anything between £20,000 and £30,000. It, of course, might be less but, as you will see, it is a very big and serious undertaking. Mrs. Schuster, who was present and is actively interested in the scheme, has the matter in hand, and I have taken the liberty of sending her your letter ... She is in touch with Captain Fraser and Lady Kitty, Miss Workman, and others of the LEAGUE and ASPADS are helping when needed. I may say that, as I have explained previously, the matter of St. Dunstan's is rather confidential at present. Whether the scheme for training these dogs will come off later or not I cannot yet say. Personally I rather doubt it. As you know, Mrs. Bond, of Skipton, has a trained blind leading dog, and she perhaps might care to give a demonstration to one or two officials of the blind institute if you get in touch with her.

The Need for Experience

Miss Crooke also wrote to Mrs. Eustis, thinking that she could recommend a book on the subject in French which she would translate for one of the Liverpool Alsatian training clubs to use. Mrs. Eustis replied cautiously on 9 July 1930.

Dear Miss Crooke,

The question of dogs as guides for the blind in England is a difficult one and I have discussed it with both Mrs. Schuster and Capt. Fraser.

I don't think any one who has not actually done the work can realize the difficulties therein encountered. It is apart from any other kind of training, as the basis must be to form a dog who takes the initiative. The man who is good at training dogs for police work usually fails with dogs for blind work as the whole principle is just the opposite.

Our great difficulty is to find men with the qualities of intelligence, patience, perception and co-ordination to succeed not only with the dogs, but with the blind. Because an instructor comes from a good school does not mean that he is a competent instructor. The very fact that he is no longer retained at a school usually indicates his inability to assimilate the requisite knowledge. The Seeing Eye therefore trains all its own instructors.

I am sorry to disappoint you, but even if there were literature on the technical questions of this training, you would learn nothing of practical value from them, because it takes the years of experience with different dogs to acquire the sense of what the dog needs to educate him as a blind guide.

I agree with you that if you could get one dog working in England it would be the opening wedge. It is what I did in America in 1927 and now we have 30 men and women with Seeing Eye dogs and 18 more being trained this summer.

I hope to be in London this September to discuss various possibilities and perhaps you could meet me there. You say Mrs. Bond who owns the only dog guide in England is going to give a demonstration with her. Has she taken the training and if not, how can she give a demonstration? It would seem like the blind leading the blind!

Is the dog the one Lady Kitty Ritson imported? If not, it is not the only dog in England. You must remember that always we have a blind man's life to consider and so the training of a dog can not be too careful. Dogs trained on the continent with right hand traffic are not safe in English left hand traffic and should be retrained. One suggestion that comes to my mind is that if you have two guide-dogs in England now, I might find someone to finance sending our assistant head instructor to England to retrain them and turn them over to two blind men.

Regretting not to be able to give you the data you want, but assuring you of our co-operation in every way.

[Further correspondence ensued, during the course of which Mrs. Eustis offered to send over, at her own expense, one of her instructors from L'Oeil qui Voit to run a trial course. By the beginning of 1931 a nucleus of four enthusiasts – Miss Crooke, Mrs. Bond, Lady Kitty Ritson and Captain Sington – were pressing on with plans for the first class, and in May they were told by Jack Humphrey, who was the manager of Mrs. Eustis's school and kennels in Switzerland, that a trainer, William Debetaz, could now be loaned from the Seeing Eye school in America. Makeshift facilities were acquired in Wallasey, at the tip of the Wirral peninsular, not far from Miss Crooke's home, and in July Humphrey came over himself to select seven dogs for the trial.

Miss Crooke recalled, in notes probably written in 1956, that when Debetaz started taking the dogs out on the streets of Wallasey in harness, he encountered mixed reactions from the public.]

The British public were completely against the idea of making a dog work, which they thought cruel. In general they had never seen such a thing. There were no dogs working for the police, army, RAF in those days, even obedience tests were comparatively rarely seen and then only at dog shows … Some people tried to stop the work. Often, and always in certain streets, Debetaz used to ask me to follow him in order to ward off these people who were such a nuisance so that he could carry on his training at all. There was one old man, the father of one of the men at the garage, who was a complete nuisance owing to his sentimental objection to dogs having to work.

Fussy Types

A letter written by Miss Crooke at the time (28 September 1931) to the secretary-general of the NIB, gives a rather more encouraging account of the situation.

Dear Mr. Eagar,

The dogs, traffic and everyday conditions don't seem to hold any unusual difficulties at all. The attitude of the public is, I think, quite all right, and on the whole kindly, particularly if they have thought Debetaz blind.

There have been a certain amount of the fussy type who like to hear their own voices who tried to say that the training was cruel, but they are practically entirely the type who have not the courage to complain to the police as they are asked to do. We have only heard of one going, and the policeman's reply was most satisfactory from our point of view and quite settled the man! Someone else complained in Liverpool that it was a wolf but as that seemed to fall flat when he went to a policeman we supposed that it was all right too.

Taken to Court

A year later (7 October 1932) there was little opposition to their activities.

Dear Mr. Eagar,

Thank you for your letter and for the copy of that other one.

The cheek of the people! Especially after a report that they put in the local paper last week! I enclose a cutting. The complaint that they speak of is the one that was made by some people in the road where the kennels are, two there, and one ever so far away. I don't remember whether you knew about it or not.

The one man makes complaints about everything and has made several people do away with their dogs and hens, and won't let children play in the road near his house. He and the other two (I rather think that someone else was behind them too) signed a noisy animals complaint paper.

As our dogs do not make enough noise to be a nuisance, and are not the only ones about there, we got a very good solicitor and when the case came up, he cross-examined these people and made fools of them, and then had the case dismissed as they had taken out the summons against the wrong person.

Though we made no defence, there would not have been much doubt about it, as we had a dozen people in court from houses near, in the road and the road behind, and papers signed by 98 people in the road and the other three roads round, to say that the guide dogs were not a nuisance.

None in those roads refused to sign.

The First Students
The five blind men that had been selected for the first course arrived in Wallasey on 3 October. One turned out to be physically unsuitable and returned home. The others were accommodated in rooms in a boarding house in Victoria Road

The four members of the first training course in October 1931: from the left, Musgrave Frankland, Allen Caldwell, Thomas ap Rhys and G.W. Lamb.

•••

and began their training. On 19 October the course was nearing completion and Jack Humphrey wrote to Miss Crooke from Switzerland.

My dear Miss Crooke,

If everything has been going according to schedule, I suppose the class there will be finishing about the time that you get this letter. I hope that everything has gone well and that the men have made satisfactory progress with their dogs. If this arrives in time, will you tell them for me to remember that when they leave they are like the boy leaving university i.e., they are not full-fledged business men but they have the basic knowledge so that they can be turned loose in the world without danger to others. Their real schooling will commence when they get home. If they will use the same care in work the first three weeks at home that I am sure Mr. Debetaz has insisted on during the course, there will be no question of their success. Tell them all they have my heartiest good wishes and that I have confidence they will not neglect the little details that make the finely finished product.

For yourself, I want to thank you for all the help you have given Mr. Debetaz while he has been there. Without you the work could not have been done. I only hope that it has been done in such a manner that you will be glad to have been connected with it and that the men will have done their work so that as they go out with their new eyes you will have a real catch in your throat as you see the shuffle gone from their feet and their heads thrown back as they take a new outlook on life. No words of mine nor of theirs can thank you for your part in helping them to such new liberty as they may find. This appreciation you will just have to realize without words and without deeds.

Glorious Freedom

Before sending William Debetaz from America to help launch the British guide dog movement, Mrs. Eustis had insisted that there should be an interval of six months to assess the results of the first trial course before making any further plans. When, in April or May 1932, the four pioneers sent in their reports, it was clear that the trial had been a success. Flash "has revolutionised my outdoor life", wrote Allen Caldwell, and continued:

Behold me now with a practically unlimited range, and able to proceed at a good, health-giving pace. Obstructions of any kind have no more terrors for me now, for Flash is so extremely sensible of my safety, consequent on her excellent training. Her piloting of me along a crowded pavement is so skilful, that it has to be seen to be believed. It is, however, in the crossing of a busy street that she is a triumph. No more unnecessary hanging about, for as soon as it is safe, off we go and often leave sighted people standing. Not only has my dog given me glorious freedom and independence, never known since pre-war days, but delightful companionship, and an unfailing friend, from whom I always receive an exuberant welcome after even a very short separation. Neither is she my dumb friend, for she communicates all manner of knowledge of which without her I should be quite unaware.

ALLEN CALDWELL,
Wallasey

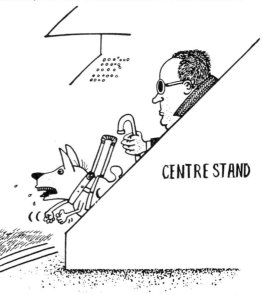

CENTRE STAND

"And **again** the early ball through the middle, and **again** the defence is caught square – and this time it's Dalglish – the shot, though, was always going high over Corrigan's bar. **But** – no doubt at **all** – that this City defence is in all **kinds** of trouble, and right now it's Liverpool who are asking all the questions!"

Folly has been my dog-guide now for some seven months. I have every confidence in her capabilities, and do not mind walking at the fastest pace or even running with her. There are just as many lamp posts and trees at the side of the pavement and people standing about in this town as any other, but Folly sees to it that I do not bump into them. She takes me down the pier daily, conducting me to the proper turnstile and negotiating all the barriers and seats that are left about. Her training in picking up anything is proving a most useful accomplishment. This was brought home to me the other day when my hat blew off. There was no one else on the pier at the time but Folly found it and brought it back quite safely ... I notice that after a very few journeys she learns to stop at a particular gate I want to turn into ... The biggest advantage of a dog-guide to a blind man accustomed to walking about alone is that all nerve strain is entirely eliminated. I can best illustrate this by saying that I am just as comfortable in my mind with or without a stick when I have Folly with me.

T. AP RHYS, Bangor

Meta is going well at present, going a nice steady pace and taking me through the crowds beautifully ... I had rather an exciting experience the other night whilst out for a walk. The pavement was in course of repair. Naturally I did not know this and when we got up to the barrier, Meta stopped and sat. People came rushing up to tell me the pavement was up; of course they were too late! I just gave her the order "left" and we went away merrily, the crowd saying what a good dog it was, and Meta seemed quite fussy too, hearing herself praised. She has indeed been a treasure ...

G.W. LAMB, Hull

Purely as a companion and the means of really healthy exercise, the dog is a real boon, and I have found Judith of immense value

Musgrave Frankland, who was secretary of the National Institute for the Blind's Liverpool branch, with his guide dog Judy. Frankland was one of the four pioneers on the first guide dog training course to be held in Britain in 1931.

to me in this respect during the past six months ... To go home after a day in a stuffy office on a still stuffier tramcar and to spend the evening in a warm room by the fire is certainly not conducive to the best of health, and to an energetic day at the office on the morrow. To be greeted at home by a dog, full of vigour and only too anxious to walk with you makes all the difference, and to have the opportunity of many miles of pleasant walking at nothing less than four miles an hour is bound to have its result, and to me, in this respect, Judith has been worth her weight in gold. I have walked with her for miles, scores of miles, down main roads with rapid motor traffic, up country roads with and without pavements, roads with awkward lamp posts, protruding trees, overhanging boughs, and I have never had the slightest mishap that could in the least reflect upon the guiding powers of Judith.

After an active sighted life, followed by dependence in many ways upon friends, the return of sight, through the eyes of

Judith, has made all the difference in the world to me, and I would not be without her for a day, and it is my earnest hope that in the near future, such help and companionship as only a guide-dog can give will be available for all who have need of such guidance.

MUSGRAVE FRANKLAND, Liverpool Secretary,
National Institute for the Blind, Liverpool Branch

The Scheme is Launched

The enthusiasm of the pioneers after six months' experience with their guide dogs provided the small nucleus of enthusiasts with all the justification that they needed to plan the next course.

Mrs. Eustis promised another trainer, on this occasion Georges Gabriel from L'Oeil qui Voit in Switzerland. "You will like him," wrote Jack Humphrey, "a very quiet and conscientious boy, speaks very little, if any, English now (fact is, he does not speak much in any language but gets along well with his blind) so you can practice your French." The prospect of a second course, and the emergence of some solid financial support, led Captain Sington to announce triumphantly that "our scheme has definitely started ... and Captain Hobbs, secretary of the Tail-Waggers Club, has taken us over as his official charity."

Gabriel arrived in England on 11 July 1932 to start training the dogs and on 15 October the second class of five blind people assembled in Wallasey. Among the four who successfully completed the course was Alfred Morgan, who worked for the Mersey Docks and Harbour Board as a clerk in the stores at the Coburg Dock yard. Morgan wrote a number of accounts of his experiences with guide dogs and the impact they had on his life, the first of which appeared in The "Tail-Wagger" Magazine in June 1933, seven months after he started his new life as a guide dog owner.

The next best thing to giving me back my eyesight was to give me Bella. My short experience of the blind world has shown me that what nearly every blind person craves for most is to be as free and independent as his sighted neighbours, or as nearly so as possible. I am no exception to the rule, and even before I got the dog I managed to get about quite nicely.

I work for the Mersey Docks and Harbour Board at the Coburg Dock Yard. The Dock Yard is at the south end of Liverpool, and I live at the north end, several miles away, and when I went back to work, some twenty months ago, after my accident [*presumably when he lost his sight*], I made use of the tramcars for the journey through the city. I did the majority of the journey by myself, but when I reached the south end, I had a guide to take me through the docks. I have to go over dock gates and bridges, and across great open spaces strewn with piles of cargo, motor lorries, railway trucks, cranes and engines of every description, and all the paraphernalia of dockland. No blind man on the face of this earth could negotiate it alone. Well, Bella and I manage very nicely, thank you. We walk through the busiest part of the town – about two miles – to one of the big city railway termini, take a train – not always from the same platform – go through six suburban stations, and toddle off home, like Darby and Joan. In fact, that is exactly what some of our fellow-passengers call us, in a friendly, amused kind of way.

At first they were simply astounded, and did not believe that I was a blind man; in fact, some of them don't believe it even now. There are people who have seen me walking through the station for the last five months who get the shock of their lives when they accidentally find out. I am not telling you this through vanity, but just to prove to those timid people who do not wish to be labelled that the possession of a guide dog does not mean that everyone takes notice of you in the streets.

From seven in the morning until eleven at night, Bella is my constant companion. She will not leave my side for a moment,

"Lovely day for a stroll, Eh!"

and follows me from room to room. At the yard she lies under my desk on a rug, and follows me round the place when I have occasion to move. She takes me about the yard, among steam lorries and travelling cranes, along narrow dock quays – we have a small private dock in the yard – and on to the river front, places that I could not possibly negotiate myself, as they are strewn with obstacles. Under these circumstances I simply put my finger under her collar, and she walks by my side and guides me perfectly. She has never let me down once. We are as regular as clockwork, and even during the snow and fog of a few weeks ago, we kept perfect time.

Then when I get home of an evening, and during the week-ends, there are the thousand and one little things one wants. To run to the post office for stamps or with one's library books, or on some small errand – I live with an elderly uncle and aunt, and there are no youngsters to do this sort of thing – or to pay a visit to friends. I just put on my hat, stretch out my hand – I know Bella is there – and off we go, anywhere, everywhere. It is just as simple as that. I know, and appreciate, and at one time even envied, the way that some blind men can get about without a dog. There is just this difference. No blind man, no matter how clever he is, can cover the ground with the ease and speed that I can, with Bella's help. Now do you see what I mean by saying that I have regained my freedom? The fact is I have another pair of eyes. It is true that I cannot see the trees and flowers, but I can most certainly see the traffic and the crowds on the pavements, and the dug-up streets, and all the obstacles one meets in a busy street. I can see the trams, trains, buses and ferry-boats – and use them whenever I have a mind to. And my guide is always there, ready and willing to take me wherever I wish to go. No waiting for someone's pleasure. Just put on my hat and off I go. And with a speed and safety that no blind man can hope for by himself.

A Taste of Freedom
Alfred Morgan was one of the more articulate of the early guide dog owners, but there were others who wrote to Miss Crooke in praise of their dogs. The three that follow are among a group of letters that were kept and used to help publicise the new training school in Wallasey.

I was going for a walk one day, and in the path there was a man-

BANX

hole. Nan took me steadily round it, there was only about two feet of room to pass, and on the other side was a drop of thirteen feet. She even picks the driest parts for me to go in, she goes in and out of pools of water and muck and she stops at the least bit of a kerb or ditch. On my way back the other day, she stopped suddenly with her nose to the ground. I gave her the command to go forward but she didn't move, so I put my hand down and to my surprise, there at my feet was a little kitten, and while handing it to a woman at the door, Nan wagged her tail, so pleased. She made sure no harm came to it. Further up the street there was a man repairing the roof of a house and he shouted out "Oi, Llewellyn, stop a minute". I smiled and calmly left it to Nan and she took me calmly round the ladder. Just before coming to it Nan was going in and out. I was told later there were workmen's tools on the pavement. Don't you think this was a thrilling experience?

R. LLEWELLYN, Rhondda Valley

I had rather a funny experience the other day. I was going to the post office at the other end of the town and was on the point of crossing a street, when a motor came along. Meta stopped, of course, waited and the motor stopped at the same time. We stayed a few minutes and then an old gentleman came trotting from the other side and told me he had stopped the motor and I could cross in safety. Meta turned her head towards me, as much as to say "What is the matter with that old fool." So I crossed and then asked him why he had stopped the motor. "Oh", he said, "I thought you would have got run over." Then I asked him not to do it again, please, and told him that my dog did not like it, and for quite two hundred yards she gave him a tottering time, because he still insisted on walking alongside. Meta kept first putting him on to the road and then on to the wall. At the finish I crossed the road to get out of his way, or else I am afraid that Meta would have done something rash, but I think it will teach him a lesson not to interfere again.

G.W. LAMB, Yorkshire

I must tell you this, I was out the other night and my dog took me between two manholes, and when I was coming back on the other side the same thing happened, and then the night watchman spoke to me, and when he found out that I could not see he was amazed, as he told me that he was watching the dog and not me, and then he showed me the holes that I had passed, as there was only just a rope around them and only three feet for me to walk on, so one side step would have seen me down one of the holes.

"Oh, sorry!"

Since I have been home with my dog I have walked along roads that I have not walked for twenty years, and I can tell you that they have changed very much from what they were. I am sure that no blind person can dream how good these dogs are until he or she has had hold of the saddle and has followed her for a few miles, as I find out that every day goes better and better, and I just walk about now as if I could see, and when I want to talk to anyone I can talk to my dog as I am sure that she knows everything that I say to her.

G.M. MATHEWS, St. Helens

A Permanent Trainer

Mrs. Eustis was persuaded to let Gabriel stay on to train a third course (his second) in the early months of 1933, and while the class was still in progress the British guide dog committee were offered the permanent trainer that they had been hoping for. Nikolai Liakhoff arrived in England in October 1933 and while he was establishing himself at Wallasey the Tail-Waggers Club were considering a request that they should take over financial responsibility for the future of guide dog training in Britain. In June 1934 they came forward with a proposal for the formation of a new organisation with an executive committee on which six of their representatives would sit with an equal number from the old guide dog committee. The proposals were accepted and on 30 August 1934 The Guide Dogs for the Blind Association was registered at Somerset House.

In the early years there was some difficulty in getting enough good applicants for guide dogs, and efforts were made to interest social workers in this new way of helping their blind clients. In the following passage, Mrs. Lucy Schuster is speaking at a Home Teachers' Conference on 3 November 1933.

I do not need to say anything about the psychology of the blind here. Some of them come to the schools depressed, hopeless, nearly suicidal. Some of them are unhealthily fat from lack of exercise or, from the same cause, suffer from sleeplessness. All are necessarily more or less dependent on human aid for guidance out of doors, or if they do get about alone can only proceed at a slow and halting pace. I think it is enough to say to you on this point that it has been proved in countries where the movement is well established that over 90 per cent. of the blind who have got these dogs have been benefited morally and physically. In many cases their whole mentality and outlook on life has been changed.

I have heard it argued that certain blind men earning a good wage prefer to pay 25s. – 30s. a week to a human guide to having

"Oh, he's a great guide. It's just keeping up with the food bills."

a guide dog, for which the only expense is his food. This seems absurd in every way. The human guide will say "goodbye" on the doorstep when he has guided his man home from work or his daily walk, and from then on the blind man must stay put or be dependent on his relations if he wants to go out. I know of one blind man with a dog who works in the Liverpool docks. He lives about six miles away. Every morning he and his dog walk about two miles through the traffic of Liverpool to the station, then his dog guides him down the station stairs to the train, takes him in the train to the docks and leads him past all the obstacles that litter a quayside, ropes, packing cases, bollards, etc. She brings him back the same way after work is over. He lives with an old uncle and aunt, and in the evening if they want an errand run he puts on his hat, puts on Bella's harness and off they go. Think of the psychological effect of this on a man to feel he is really independent and not a burden but a boon to his relatives. I could give you many similar instances if time allowed, but I hope perhaps you will go and see for yourselves. In the south of England we have men with dogs in Barnes and Southampton, and I shall be delighted to give the names and addresses to anyone who is interested in seeing them work.

I have told you a little of what we are setting out to do; now I want to ask you if you will help us. A west end hospital very sensibly had in large letters on its walls "Help is better than sympathy." We do want your help. It is through your sympathetic co-operation and through that only that we shall be able to get the right sort of blind to use these dogs. We want you to tell the blind in your charge of this movement and to dispel their prejudices, which are, I think, usually groundless and born of ignorance. We want you to recommend candidates for our dogs; men and women that you with your experience will know to be suitable for them, but most of all we want your sympathy. We want to feel that the associations for the blind are working with us in our effort to bring "light to them that sit in darkness".

[By 1934, with the help of the NIB and Home Teachers, the difficulty in recruiting good applicants was over. There were now "heaps of blind people wanting dogs" according to Miss Crooke, "far more than we can supply." Many of these applicants were young, civilian blind people, who had previously been greatly outnumbered by men from St. Dunstan's.]

✶ Chapter Two ✶

THE JOY OF INDEPENDENCE

In the years before the Second World War most blind people were forced to live very much more sheltered lives than they do today. Not only were there few educational and employment opportunities, but the only mobility aids were a human guide or a white walking stick with which to feel the way along a wall or kerb.

It is hardly surprising, therefore, that guide dogs brought about a profound revolution in the lives of the relatively small number of people who could be provided with them in the early years. They were not always received with enthusiasm, however. About three weeks after the end of the fourth training course one of the participants, probably Mr. A. Gaffney, a St. Dunstaner living in St. Helens, returned to Wallasey and asked Miss Crooke to take the dog back. In fact, Miss Crooke recorded, "he had been sent by his wife with a note asking me to do so. Trouble at home, he had become so independent and was able to go anywhere at any time that he liked, and did so, so she was jealous and threatened to leave him." As Miss Crooke commented, the wife's action was a great compliment to the dog and its owner, who had further demonstrated their skill by travelling through Liverpool and across the Mersey on the ferry to the training centre on their own. The matter seems to have been resolved by Miss Crooke sending him home with a letter for his wife, followed up by a visit with the new trainer, Nikolai Liakhoff. Thereafter, the guide dog and its owner continued working together until May 1936, when the dog was sold as a pet because, according to Miss Crooke,

•••

"Gaffney says he could no longer afford to keep and feed her."

Gaffney's experience was not common but, as the first item below demonstrates, it was not an isolated phenomenon of the early pioneer years.

The remaining passages, however, bear witness to the joys of owning a guide dog.

Adverse Criticism
From the Association's journal, Forward, *December 1944.*
A guide dog owner recently wrote to Capt. Liakhoff, sending him a copy of a letter he had received from an old girl friend. The matter is a little too personal for us to be able to print the letter in its original form. But we give it below, with the names altered. It is meant to be critical of guide dogs, and what they do for blind people. Yet in that criticism there is an unconscious tribute to the independence that a guide dog can give to a blind man. And we hope that you will get a smile out of it – as we did.
"Dear Archibald," the letter began.

"You will perhaps think it strange that I should write to you but as you will see I have a reason for doing so.

"I well remember the day in 1940 when you told me you were going for a dog. You talked of a new life which the dog would open for you. I could not see what was wrong with the old one! After your training you came back a changed man! My friends said it was a change for the better, but I don't think it was. You were not your old self. You found new sighted friends and you did not take things for granted like you used to do. You forgot about your old blind friends and even when I wanted to take you somewhere you had always got that damn dog with you. That dog hated me, and what girl wants a man who is more fond of his dog than her?

"They spoiled you over there. Instead of the nice quiet boy

you were, you now talk out of your turn. Think of it, you might have had a wife to look after you instead of this so-called new life.

"Now for my reason for writing to you. Since I gave you up for the sake of that dog I have got a new boy friend. He is John Smith, a young man who has only been blind a year. The other day I found out from his parents that you had been talking to them about guide dogs. If you have a heart left in you please leave John alone. He and his parents were impressed by what you said and did to show them the work of the dogs.

"Archibald, I hated what they did to you! I shall break my heart if John gets like you. If that man left you a heart you tell John not to have a dog after all!"

The First Meeting
From Emma and I *by Sheila Hocken, 1977.*

In the lounge [of the training centre] after breakfast the following day there was tremendous expectancy and excitement because we all knew we were going to meet our dogs for the first time. Brian gave us a final briefing, and then asked us to go back to our rooms. "There'll be less distraction there," he said, "and you'll get to know your dog, and vice versa, with a bit of peace and quiet."

I went up to Number Ten – able to find my way now unaided. I sat on the edge of the bed waiting, with the door open, and with enough time to have a stray, disturbing thought: what if my dog doesn't like me? What if she stands growling at me? Then I heard Brian's footsteps approaching along the corridor, and with them I heard the clicking patter of a dog's paws.

"Here we are, Sheila," said Brian as he came into the room, "here's your dog. She's called Emma, and she's a chocolate-coloured Labrador."

At the same time I heard a tail swishing the air, and Brian leaving, closing the door behind him. "Emma," I called.

Sponsored walk through Nottingham.

Immediately she came bounding across the room, and suddenly I was nearly bowled off the bed.

Then I was licked all over. "Hello, Emma," I said, "hello." I could hardly believe it. She kept licking me, and pushing her cold nose into my hands. I knew then we were going to get on together. She likes me, I thought. She likes me. I could have danced round the room.

I tried to feel the shape of her head, but she would not stop bouncing up and down in front of me, twisting, turning and making snuffling noises in my hands. Every now and then I got a wet nose in my face. But at last she settled and sat by my feet, and I was able to feel what she was like. Her coat was very thick and rough, reminding me of a Teddy bear's. She was smallish for a Labrador, not fat, but thickset. She had a very thick tail, and ears that were as soft as velvet. And she was so lively.

Emma did not give me long to run my hands over her. She started to fetch me things. Under the dressing table I kept my shoes. She began rushing after them, and bringing them to me one by one. The message was quite clear. "Here I am. I'm Emma. I'm your new dog, and this is your gift, a shoe." I could not remember ever being so happy before. And from those first few moments of greeting, Emma's affection has never wavered. From then on she was never to leave my side, and I, in turn, took on the responsibility for her every need.

Home Again
Also from Emma and I.

All too soon the day came when we were to go home, Emma and I. It was, oddly enough, very sad. It happened to be raining – pouring down – and the weather matched my mood. Even though I could not see the rain, I felt very grey and depressed. I hated the idea of having to leave the centre and all the friends I had made. Even more, I really did not want to go home, although I now had Emma, and kept trying to convince myself that things back in Nottingham were bound to be different. I was afraid that somehow I might be enveloped in the old ways again, despite Emma. I had not yet grasped to what an enormous extent she was about to change my life. I still had to learn to put my confidence in her.

"Understanding between man and dog quickly develops ... !"

Heavy with misgivings, I left Leamington with Emma in her harness beside me. The two of us arrived in Nottingham, were met and taken home. Once home, I let Emma off the lead and took off her harness: she went wild. Everyone was immediately taken with her. She bounded all over the place, through every room, round and round; I could hear her tearing about, sending rugs flying, stopping to sniff each chair and table leg. The air swished to the wagging of her tail, and resounded with her snortings and sniffings. This, she obviously realised, was where she was going to live.

It was such a different Emma from the sober responsible animal on the harness, and for the first time I appreciated that there were two distinct sides to her character: one when she was working, and in charge of me, and the other when she was off the harness, totally joyous, full of fun and energy, and as far from any sense of responsibility as a clown. My misgivings began to evaporate.

That first night back, Emma slept at the bottom of the bed; she had decided that there was no other place good enough for her, and in the morning she woke me with her usual insistence. It struck me that this morning we were really starting a new life together. We would be going out into Nottingham on our own. I got out of bed and started dressing. This was not my usual form, because I'm normally a very slow, sleepy starter, but on this day of all days I could not wait to find out how Emma and I, put to the test, would get on together.

Over breakfast I decided we would go to visit some old friends, Norman and Yvonne, whom I hadn't seen recently and who lived quite near. In the decision itself lay the prospect of freedom. With Emma, I would be able to go all over Nottingham!

I had the directions worked out in my mind after a telephone consultation. They presented no problems: all I had to do was to go out of our front gate, tell Emma to turn right to the top of the road, a main road, turn right again, go straight to the bottom, turn left, and ask Emma to find the first gate. So, off we went.

Twenty minutes after setting out, we were standing in the porch of Norman and Yvonne's house, and I was feeling for the bell. We had done it. To anyone walking down that Nottingham street of detached houses, lined with trees and built in the 1920s, there may have appeared nothing out of the ordinary about a girl and a dog standing in a doorway waiting for the bell to be answered. But inside me was a huge sense of triumph: it was a milestone. "Good girl, Emma," I kept saying. I was so proud of her.

Norman and Yvonne were naturally delighted to see me, and they were even more thrilled to meet Emma. They made a great fuss of her. Several hours later we set off home and found our way back to the main road. Then came a terrible realization. In my excitement that everything was going so well with Emma, I had forgotten to count how many intersections we had crossed.

There had been no need to count on the way there because we went as far as the road went, up to a T-junction. But I should have counted for getting back. And I hadn't. So there I was with no idea where I should tell Emma to turn left. After a whole month of training, I had straightaway forgotten one of the cardinal principles: always count the roads as you go.

What could I do? I thought: Here I am, and there's no trainer to save me.

Emma, all unknowing, was taking me along at her furious pace, and I felt I had let Emma down. I seemed alienated from her through my own eagerness and thoughtlessness; I was sure, too, that she would never commit a mistake that would put us both in jeopardy. Emma wasn't in the least daunted, however, and, ignoring my commands, started taking me down a side road. I tried to stop her. "No, Emma. No! Go back, go back!" But she paid no attention. In turn, I dared not let go of her, so I had to follow. At last she turned left again, and sat down. Instinctively I put my hand out. I felt leaded-lights and painted wood with one or two blisters. It was my back door. If I had forgotten to count the roads on the way out, Emma certainly hadn't!

Sally Comes Home
David Scott-Blackhall in Forward, 1960.

When I returned home with Sally, it was not only the first time in all my life that I had had a dog but it was the first time, in twenty-four years of married life, that we had had a pet of any kind. The family, of which the Alsatian became the latest

member, consists of my wife and myself and our two daughters, Jane aged nineteen and Susan aged eleven.

Looking back, I remember that I had to be talked into

having a guide dog. I was put off partly because of my lack of knowledge about dogs and, more especially, by the sentimentality one often finds among so-called dog-lovers. Sally is immeasurably valuable to me and I am very fond of her, but I shall not do her the disservice of investing her with human qualities. I shall avoid talking to her in baby language!

Shortly after we came home together, I heard each of my daughters giving her own version of why I had acquired a guide dog. "You see," Jane explained to one of her friends, "Daddy likes to be waited on. One day he called Mummy, who was in the kitchen, and she didn't come at once because she was busy. When she came, Daddy thought he would like to pretend that he is the boss, so he told Mummy that when he called her, he didn't want her to come when she thought she would. He wanted her to drop everything and come bounding up with a cry. What you need, answered Mummy, is an Alsatian. So Daddy went and got one!"

Susan's account was different, but equally imaginative. "You know why Daddy has a guide dog, instead of his daughters, to take him for walks?" she asked, rhetorically. "Because Mummy can't ask Sally where they've been."

In the dog world, I think it is not too fanciful to say that the working dogs are the aristocrats. It is a constant source of wonder to me that Sally can be bounding and frisking in the garden like a playful kitten, yet as soon as I call her she comes eagerly – just like Jane said Mummy is supposed to do. And once in the harness she ceases to be a playful kitten and becomes as sedate as an archbishop. She is by no means the one-man-dog which Alsatians are reputed to be, but she will cheerfully and readily desert any member of the family when she hears the rattle of her lead.

Once, in the height of the summer, I was having breakfast wondering why the dog had not yet greeted me. I assumed that she was playing in the garden.

"It's a revolutionary new idea we're trying."

"I don't think she is," my wife told me. "I'll go and see if I can find her." She came back almost exploding with laughter and I learned that Susan had discovered a new use for Sally. With the lead fully extended, she had put it on the dog, donned her roller skates, and Sally had been pulling her at high speed along the pavement. Susan was not the only one who enjoyed it, from all accounts!

I live in a quiet, suburban road, about 150 yards from the junction with the main road. I always take the opportunity, as soon as I reach the home straight, of loosening up by running the last 150 yards.

This is an exercise which Sally greatly enjoys, although I am not sure whether such undignified behaviour would not be frowned on by the Association. They certainly did not teach us anything about running, down at Exwick! Fortunately, mine is a wide pavement with no lamp-posts.

One gets asked a lot of stupid questions about the dog, and some people would not be surprised if I told them that Sally had been trained to make a pot of tea. A few days ago, I was stopped by a man who apparently wanted to admire the dog. "What's his name?" he asked me. Put in that way, it is rather a difficult question to answer. "His name is Sally," I answered, trying not to make it sound sarcastic.

"I suppose he – she is trained to protect you if anyone should attack you?"

"Do you think anyone is likely to attack me?" I asked. "You never know," he persisted. "But I suppose that's all part of her training." "She is a guide dog," I said, "not a police dog."

But my tenacious friend would not let go. "Still," he reasoned, "I reckon if someone did attack you, she would protect you." "Tell you what," I suggested, "let's put your theory to the test. You hit me and we'll see what she does." There was a moment's silence and, for a horrible moment, I wondered whether my enthusiastic friend was going to take me at my word.

Then, "No thanks," he said, and passed out of my life.

Sally is a perplexing mixture of intelligence and stupidity. Almost invariably, she prefers to lie across the threshold of the room, so that she receives a buffet every time the door is opened. She gets under my feet at home and office, so that I fall over her several times a day. When I am typing or using the Braille machine, she has a habit of lumbering up and pushing her face underneath my arm, emitting an un-Alsatian-like squeal. I have yet to discover what this means. If I know Sally, it means nothing in particular, except perhaps "How do you do?" I have a blanket in the corner of my office where she sits down, morning and afternoon, but she always gets up to exchange a few pleasantries with everyone who comes into the office. No use to tell her to go and lie down. I have to get up and show her where it is and tell her to come and lie down.

My monthly report gives the information that Sally's obedience, out of harness, is moderately good. This is the only item which gives rise to any comment. But she is so good-natured, so amiable a dog, and so splendid at the work for which she is primarily intended, that I can shrug off these small lapses.

She attracts to herself the admiration of friends and strangers and, when this happens, I feel a strange pride, as if the credit were mine. On several occasions, she has taken me from my home to Broadcasting House, twelve miles away, and sat in the studio with me during a recording session, without making the least sound. On the last occasion, two girls travelled in the lift with Sally and me, and one of them said: "We don't often have a fellow-traveller as handsome as this." For some reason which I can't explain, I knew she didn't mean me!

Change Of Direction
David Scott-Blackhall in The Way I See It *(1971).*
After a long lecture trip, we alighted, Sally and I, at Kings Cross station, and I hadn't taken particular notice which way the train

was travelling. Consequently, I half turned away from the barrier as we stepped down from the train. "If that's the way you want to go, all right then," said Sally. I suddenly realised that all the other passengers were walking in the opposite direction. Without altering my pace, I spoke very deliberately, my voice about an octave lower than usual: "You are a very stupid dog." That was all she needed.

David Scott-Blackhall with Sally.

"I thought a nip of brandy would keep us both warm."

She wheeled round, abruptly but with the utmost grace, as if this is what she had intended to do from the first, and we retraced our steps, going roughly one and a half times as fast. "I wondered where you were going," said one of the passengers as I overtook him.

Weight-Watching
The next two passages are also from David Scott-Blackhall's book.

On one occasion, I went into a pub with Sally and one of the customers was admiring her. "Can I give her a bar of chocolate?" he asked me.

"I'd rather you didn't," I said courteously. "She doesn't have chocolate."

"A bar of chocolate won't hurt her," he insisted. "It's only two ounces."

I was quite unruffled and smiling about it. "I'm sorry," I said, "I go into so many places and everybody wants to feed her. I have to watch her weight. She is fed once a day at a regular time."

That was the end of it, I would have thought, but Sally had stood up and seemed to be fidgeting.

"Come on now, lie down!" I said.

"She's all right," said the stranger, "she's just finished the chocolate."

"You weigh seventeen stone six pounds."

This is a genuine incident, exactly like that, and similar things have happened at other times. I sometimes feel that I ought to have thrown my glass of beer into the face of my clever friend but that would only have taught him a lesson and it was unlikely that I would ever meet him again. At the time, I said nothing further. I drained my glass and left.

Sally would take me into Boots, so that she could be weighed on the orthodox penny-in-the-slot machine. There was a kind of ritual about it.

It is a fairly big shop and there were always plenty of customers but everything stopped while Sally was weighed. The assistant stood by the machine with my penny in her hand as I removed the harness. It was at this stage that the world stood still. There would be a chorus of murmurs from the customers in all parts of the shop.

"Look, he's going to weigh the dog."

"Ah, look at that!"

"Aaaah!"

The first few visits, I had to plant Sally's front paws on the far corner of the weighing platform before lifting her hind-quarters onto the diagonal corner. After that, she always knew where to put her front paws but, for the benefit of the spectators, I took the trouble to tell her. I had to be careful that she didn't beat me to it.

"Put your front paws on that corner," I said, pointing. Sally, as if understanding, was clambering into Position Number One. The gallery caught its breath.

"Aaaah!" they said.

I placed my hand on the top of her paws for a moment. "Keep them there," I said sternly. Then I lifted her back legs and sat her on the platform.

The assistant stood with penny poised against the slot.

"Don't put it in until I tell you," I said. "Stay, Sally, staaay!" Her tail was dangling on the floor, I lifted it up and curled it onto the scale. "No cheating," I said firmly. A little appreciative chuckle from my audience. I held up my hand to the assistant while I made my final inspection. Everything was still and silent, patrons and staff holding their breath. "Now!" I said. The penny rattled down and the assistant inspected the dial. "Five stone ten," she announced slowly. I yanked Sally off the scale. "You fat pig!" I said.

"Aaaah!" One of these days, I thought, we shall get a round of applause.

It's different with Honor. The first time the ritual was exactly the same as before. I coaxed her front paws onto the corner of the platform and then lifted her into a sitting position on the scale. The second time, as soon as I had removed her harness, she climbed on to the platform and sat down. The carnival was over. No more elaborate playing to the gallery.

Mistaken Identity

Sally and I walked from Broadcasting House to Baker Street and there I caught the Green Line Coach, forty minutes from home. So that the dog would not be too much in the way, I went to the back of the bus, a single decker, and sat in an empty double seat. Sally used to assume that she was entitled to jump up on to the seat, if there was a spare one, so I always took care to settle her firmly in the gangway, with muttered threats of dire consequences. In spite of this, after three or four stops, there was a plop on the seat beside me. I immediately thrust out my hand to push her off, and the same time growling impressively, "Get down!" My hand rested, not on a hairy Alsatian, but on a trousered leg.

"I beg your pardon," I said hurriedly, "I thought you were my dog." I was answered by a deep and rather cultured voice. "I know,

POST OFFICE

"Come on boy, lead me home."

it's the shape of my ears. I'm often mistaken for an Alsatian."

I thought this was an exceedingly comic remark in the circumstances, and I tried desperately to think of a witty riposte. "It might be worse," was all I could think of. "It might have been a young lady I was trying to push off the seat." My companion sounded as if he was going to speak and then seemed to check himself. I felt we were at cross-purposes somehow, but I couldn't fathom out what was wrong.

Someone called out from lower down the coach, "I've got your ticket Marjorie".

"Thank you," said my companion with the Alsatian ears. She said it in a rather subdued voice, as if she didn't want someone to know that she was the one who had been addressed.

It was a thousand miles to Borehamwood and I couldn't think of anything to say.

Adventures On The Underground
R. Stevenson in Forward, 1967.

Shane, although still a youngster, is quite a large dog, standing about three feet tall and weighing nearly seventy pounds. As I change at Holborn from the Piccadilly Line to the Central, I have to pick him up and carry him up the escalator. This doesn't worry him at all and he stays quite relaxed in my arms and enjoys the ride. A couple of weeks ago we had completed the trip uneventfully, but when I squatted to replace his feet on the ground I split my trousers up the back seam. The accident happened when I was halfway down and I didn't know whether to continue my descent and risk total exposure, or to rise, still with Shane in my arms, and retreat backwards to the nearest wall and rob the tittering young ladies spilling off the escalator behind me of a sight never-to-be-forgotten. My blushes were spared, however, when a gallant gentleman came to my rescue, standing behind me whilst I hastily donned a pack-a-mac which I fortunately had with me. Needless to say, I have now developed a new technique for returning Shane to the ground, and incid-entally, have advised the powers that be at Exeter for future reference.

"What's the problem?"

Shane has improved so much lately that I can now leave my home in Hertfordshire, and without giving him any directions whatsoever, can complete the journey to my office in the West End in complete safety. He will en route find the steps leading down to the underground station, go through the ticket barrier and find the door of the guard's compartment.

• •

Alighting at Holborn he will take me from the platform to the foot of the escalator, from the top of which he will take me to the steps going down to the Central Line and once again will find his own way to the fixed centre stairway, 150 steps in all, and lead me, breathless by now, past the ticket collector who sympathetically returns my panted "… morning," straight to the front door of the building in which I work. Once inside, he settles quietly on his bed beside me and hardly stirs till I break off for lunch, when he is up like a rocket the instant I remove my headset from the switchboard. After lunch and a run in the nearby gardens, he returns to his bed where he stays until about three o'clock when he is wakened by the sound of teacups and the promise of a forbidden snack. Contrary to my strict instructions that no tit-bits are to be given, some forgetful person will leave a piece of cake on the desk – two feet nine as opposed to Shane's three feet – then quick as a flash Shane is gazing contentedly from his bed at one hungry typist. Even the Manager is no exception, and his favourite piece of fruit cake suffered the same fate recently.

What a difference Shane has made to my life already. No longer do I sit in the office at midday envying those who could get out into the fresh air, for I can now set off to where my fancy takes me. The regular trip to my barber which I often put off until I was shamed into making it, I now regard as a pleasant jaunt. The bottle of iced lager so often fancied on a hot day is no longer out of reach, but at my finger tips in a matter of minutes. I am able to lighten my wife's load by calling at one or two of the shops on my way home. Also, something which I have longed to do for a number of years is to attend evening classes in order that I may take the City and Guilds examination on radio theory, and eventually, I hope, to take out a GPO licence to transmit. This task I have never had the courage to attempt on my own because of the difficulty of getting to the class, but with Shane's help it is now a reality. Not only does he take me to the school, which is situated some eight miles from my home, but he also takes me straight to the classroom door.

The First Days
From an article by Miss Mary Melling
in The "Tail-Wagger" Magazine, *July 1939.*
Going home with your guide dog is a very exciting business for a blind person. And no wonder! For you are either regaining your lost freedom, or you are literally tasting freedom for the first time! In either case, it means you are starting life all over again ... and your world seems wonderful beyond words!

I shall never forget my first days home with my dog Mandy. At that time, my knowledge of our local geography was of the

Miss Mary Melling and Mandy, Winter 1934.

haziest: so I had to content myself just pottering about near home, gradually extending my walks until I could go for several miles without getting lost. Whenever possible, I would get a general idea of my route before starting out, and if necessary ask as I went. Often, though, I didn't do even that, but just went wandering along unfamiliar roads, for the sheer joy of finding out where they led to.

And I can still feel the thrill of wandering for the first time, through our local parks and gardens, threading my way between the flower-beds, absolutely unaccompanied save by Mandy! It was early Spring, and birds were singing everywhere, and the scent of wallflowers filled the air ... and to me it seemed like a fairy tale come true!

Yet first days home with your guide dog are not all child's play, far from it! For whereas, at Wallasey, you had the help of Captain Liakhoff and Miss Crooke, now there isn't anyone who even vaguely understands ... yet everybody everywhere wants to help you. Indeed, this would-be helpfulness on the part of passers-by is easily the most difficult thing you ever have to deal with. And there doesn't seem very much you can do about it ... if only for the sake of others less fortunate than yourself, who may be in actual need of such assistance.

Gradually, however, as you and your dog grow more and more accustomed to one another, this interference affects you less and less. But just at first, it does seem rather desperate.

Healthier and Happier
by Andrew Gilzean, The "Tail-Wagger" Magazine, March 1936.
I don't know what I would do without Lady nowadays. I don't think that I could exist without her. I feel so much healthier and happier since I got her. I was rather surprised some time ago when we were discussing Lady at home. My mother said there was a

Andrew Gilzean and Lady, Spring 1935.

great difference now in the way I go about the house, and that I very seldom had "that worried, anxious expression". I had always thought I got about the house at least quite well, and that I seldom looked anxious or nervous, but it appears I was wrong.

As Good as a Holiday

Part of a letter written in 1934 by Miss Mary Melling.

Mother and I are still busy, too – with Mandy's numerous admirers! We never knew how many friends we had until now. In addition to our entertaining here, we are also being invited out – so long as we take Her Ladyship with us … Mandy certainly is causing a sensation in this quarter of the globe. The other morning she took me right round a fire in the middle of the pavement. She doesn't care about fire, as you probably know, yet she never took me out into the road, and the pavement wasn't particularly wide either, so doesn't she take care of me? To tell you the truth, I don't know what on earth I should do without her. She is just about the finest pal anyone ever had. I am fairly revelling in my new- found freedom. I am now exploring all sorts of roads I have never been along before. If I don't know where a road leads to, I just go along to see. It is as good as a holiday, believe me. And what a joy walking is now. I am walking farther and farther all the time, and each day is happier than the last. Mandy is enjoying it too. One look at her tail when I pick up her harness would be sufficient to tell you that.

Christmas Shoppers

From a letter by Miss Mary Melling to Captain Alan Sington, published in The "Tail-Wagger" Magazine, *August 1937.*

I think the greatest thrill I have had this winter was mingling with the Christmas shoppers, unaccompanied save for a dog! It is a bit of a thrill, you know. Going along Princes Street in a Christmas crowd, without receiving so much as a jolt, is no mean achievement, believe me. And we don't go along slowly either! But when we turn to come home I always think she really excels herself. She will pause at all the appropriate places, just in case I might wish to do something unexpected: but provided I say nothing, she just goes on again, and will take me home without a single command of any kind.

I am not allowed to pass any friends in the street, and they have often had to come across to me from the opposite side of the street, because I have refused point blank to cross, not knowing

her reason. My friends are always very pleased about this, for they say one does not expect such things of other people's dogs.

As a matter of fact, Mandy is a tremendous favourite with everybody. I couldn't tell you how many complete strangers, let alone friends, have come up to me, remarking that this is the very first time they have ever wanted to pet an Alsatian, and I have simply had to let them, if only to break down the common prejudice against the breed. Fortunately it doesn't affect Mandy's work, and it does make her so much more welcome on cars and buses.

The Travelling Preacher
by Rev. Glyn Thomas, in Forward, *1954.*

My life is a very busy one. Visiting, travelling, studying and preaching. I am a resident minister of a church, but get many calls to various churches and chapels in other towns and cities.

Since I lost my sight I have carried on my work, but oh! the fuss when I was going to a new place, or to preach for a week-end at another church. Someone looking up trains, telegrams, instructions; someone to take me to the station; someone to meet me at the other end. Handed from one to another as carefully as if I were a bit of china and would break if let go of! I was grateful for this help; but oh, how many times I wished for freedom and liberty.

Then I applied for a guide dog; and after a period of waiting, and then of training, I arrived home with my new eyes, "Patch". He was great.

Together we travelled England and Wales. No more fuss and bother for other people – I was free, and could go about like any sighted person. We learned where the different shops were, and could even help at home by doing the shopping. No longer need to wait until someone had time to take me visiting. Off we would go, Patch and I! He knew the homes of my church members, and always, as a good parson does, he enjoyed a cup of tea with me when we arrived at one.

Then disaster came my way. The Monday before Christmas, 1952, while out with a friend, I let Patch loose for a run on a grass verge. Within three seconds he was knocked down and killed! The days that followed were dark days. Friends and relations sympathised and did all they could to help, but they could not understand. Patch had become part of me. He was my eyes, and it was as if I was blinded again to be without him. All the glorious independence was gone. I was again relying on other people. How I longed for my dear Patch! But how I needed another guide dog.

Soon I was sent for again, to train with a replacement.

Could he be as good as Patch? Would we become a team like Patch and I had been? With dogs, as with humans, some friendships can be closer and more understanding than others. These were my thoughts as I travelled.

All this wondering left me, however, when I was introduced to "Kim", my new eyes. Oh, the thrill when I felt the handle of the harness again; and, as the training went on, realised that we should be alright together.

Nothing can ever eclipse Patch's memory, or lessen my sorrow at his tragic end; but I am fortunate enough to be able to say that, in our travelling together, Kim is proving his worthy successor.

It does not matter if the railway carriage is empty, I am never lonely, for Kim will keep touching me in a friendly way, and I know I have a friend who will not fail. No loneliness when travelling; no difficulties when we alight. Kim knows the barriers and takes me straight to them, till I hear "tickets please". Then through we go. Outside the station we ask for directions, and I pass them on to Kim. Never have we failed to arrive safely at our destination.

In the services Kim behaves himself splendidly and, like many church-goers, sleeps through the sermon.

When the service is over I say "Home Kim!" and he promptly takes me back to our lodgings. This is amazing, as we have only been there once to leave our luggage; but he knows we are staying there, and he takes me straight back to the house. He never offers to take me to the station until I have packed my bag and am leaving my host. Then again I say "Home Kim!" and this time he makes for the station without any hesitation.

We are well-known in the hospitals here, as we go visiting. Kim gets to know the patients we visit, and takes me straight to the right bed when I say the name. He is a most friendly dog, and makes many friends for me as we go along.

The Little Things
by Miss O. White, in Forward, *June 1948.*
We were coming home from the office one day, when we came to a greengrocer's lorry parked half on the road and half on the rather narrow pavement in front of the chapel. The other half of the pavement was taken up by the greengrocer's customers, and there was a lot of traffic on the road. So, as a last resort, Roy turned into the big gate of the chapel, walked behind the railing in safety, and came out through the little gate.

He could see both gates from the pavement, and fortunately they were both open. In this way we passed the lorry and the customers without having to worry about traffic. It made the other people laugh, but I was rather puzzled until someone told me what Roy had done.

Perhaps Roy thinks I should go to chapel more often. Not every dog would think of his mistress's soul as well as her body.

Roy goes in for the pleasures of the mind as well as the pleasures of the body. Whenever I put down his food he stands looking at it, licking his mouth, and then eats it slowly; but he seems to get as much pleasure out of the anticipation as he does out of the food itself.

I was trying to think out the other evening why having a guide dog should have made such a difference to me. Really, it's the little things that matter, isn't it? – being able to cross a busy road without having to draw attention to oneself by asking for help, and lots of things like that.

Making Friends ...
by W.V. Jones, in Forward, December 1947.

Mick himself can hardly be styled sociable, for friendly advances to him, except in the case of a favoured few, are usually met with a quiet aloof dignity. Nevertheless his presence provides me with a sure passport of acceptance into a gathering of people. So many sighted people are shy with the blind; nervous, maybe, and so afraid of saying the wrong thing that they will say nothing at all, while others, with would-be kindliness, speak in a bluff, too hearty manner and in loud voice as though the blind were necessarily deaf as well. For years I found this self-consciousness, on my part and theirs, a very limiting factor in my relations with other people, but with the coming of Mick it is as though a barrier had been broken down.

All the world, or nearly so, it seems to me, loves the dog; always I find there is a friendly greeting for Mick; conversation will start naturally and without constraint because someone is always ready to talk about my dog or his dog or dogs in general, and the conversation once begun will go from one topic to another. We exchange views and offer suggestions on the weather, our hobbies, our gardens or the political situation with equal ease; in fact I feel that I am accepted as "one of the party".

But it is not only of ordinary social gatherings that I am thinking. On Sunday mornings Mick comes with me to church where his behaviour is exemplary. (He stands when the congregation stands and lies down when we kneel or sit). It is significant to me that for ten years at least I have attended this church with a human guide and have scarcely exchanged a word with other members of the congregation. Now, as we come out, nearly everyone has a word to say, either to Mick or to me or to both of us, and I certainly know that in these last few months of church-going I have met with more real fellowship than in all the years before.

... and Influencing People
by Phyllis Townsend, in Forward 1975.

Quite soon after World War Two, a little blind girl came as a pupil to the Bristol Royal School for the Blind where I was teaching. She was a Polish girl but was afraid and suspicious of everyone and her particular dread was my guide dog Ruff. If she heard Ruff bark, this little girl would race from the room screaming in absolute terror.

In vain, everyone told her that the dog would not hurt her. I tried to keep Ruff away from her for a while till she had settled down a bit. I was sad about this, realising that when this girl grew up she would find a guide dog so helpful in mobility, but I felt rather helpless about it.

Then Ruff took the situation in hand. In class, if this little girl was there, Ruff would lie at her feet or sit quietly beside her. Gradually, the child began to have the dog near her without making a fuss so long as it was quiet.

It was quite noticeable to other people as well as myself that Ruff seemed to make a point of singling this girl out however many other children were around.

The final stage of this conquest was on a coach-outing when Ruff went to the length of her leash and sat down beside the girl on the coach. The girl didn't know she was there for a while but when she discovered her she began to stroke her rather cautiously. Ruff kept perfectly still and sat beside her all the way as I had a quiet running commentary on this from a sighted friend of mine on the staff. On the return journey from the seaside, where we had spent the afternoon, Ruff again sat beside the girl and towards the end of the journey back to school Ruff was resting her head on the little girl's knee. After this, they were complete friends. The girl, when old enough, qualified in examinations to go to a college.

About a year after this success I met her at the National Library for the Blind in London when her first words were, "Where's Ruff?" I replied, "Lying under the grand piano." Down went the girl on hands and knees under the piano in search of Ruff. The re-union was touching with Ruff ending up kissing her face. There is a finale to this story, which is perfectly true. One day this young lady's name appeared in a list of new guide dog owners. Her name is Miss Danuta Blawat who recently qualified at Forfar with Alma. I could almost wish her dog was named Ruff, as my second guide dog Ruff conquered where humans failed.

A Life of Her Own

Taken from an article by May Sabeston Walker in The Road to Freedom, *a pamphlet published by the Association in 1944.*

"Now isn't that sad!" I said to Don, as we walked briskly down the main road to do our shopping, and although his response was one of silent consent I knew by the wag of his feathery tail and by the slight quickening of his pace that he agreed with what I had said.

The reason for my remark was that we had just passed a blind man, tap-tapping his way along with his white stick.

May Sabeston Walker with her first guide dog Wendy in 1937.

A kind lady, with a great deal of fuss, had helped him to cross the road safely; and with many words of thanks and assurance that he would now be able to carry on alone, he had managed to free himself from his helper and to continue slowly and conspicuously on his way.

Meanwhile Don and I had ourselves crossed the same road quite unnoticed, and had very soon left behind the blind man with his stick. Yet I continued to hear the tap-tap in my imagination, and to think rather sadly of the owner of the stick.

Then it occurred to me that it was strange that I, who am myself without sight, should be thinking so pityingly of a blind person, when I had always intensely disliked being pitied by other people.

"I suppose," I thought to myself, "that the reason is that I am no longer blind. It is true that I haven't the sight of my own eyes, but I have a guide dog and he has given me the 'second sight' which makes it possible for me to lead so normal a life that I no longer live like a blind person, or even think of myself as one."

It is not only my body that has acquired freedom of

movement, but my mind also. A blind person can become so accustomed to consulting the wishes of the human guide upon whom he is so dependent that in the long run he may lose the ability to make his own decision, so that even his mental outlook leans upon that of other people.

To many blind people guide dogs have restored the sight they once possessed. But I was born blind, and to me a guide dog has given the sight which I have never known.

It is no wonder that I agreed wholeheartedly with the small boy who trotted up to me one day whilst I was walking with my guide dog, and remarked with the wisdom of youth, "You was blind once, wasn't you?"

A Complete Partnership

by Alfred Swede, also from The Road to Freedom. *For the first few months after he lost his sight Alfred Swede was busy learning to read and write braille.*

But as the days wore on – and sometimes they seemed never-ending – I took less interest in everyday things; idleness and lack of responsibility began to fray my nerves. I slept restlessly and woke listlessly, for there was nothing to look forward to.

Everybody was kind to me. As the months went by I learned with bitterness to loathe the idea of "sympathy". I got it from all sides.

I once tried to walk with the aid of a white stick – they said "If only you got yourself out and about you'd feel a different man" – and was like a toddler who could walk with confidence only by touching another human being. I quickly lost sense of direction, bumped hard into things, and it was only through the kindness of some children, who placed me squarely on the pavement, that I reached home with my bruises and a firm resolve that never again would I venture out alone. From that moment I knew I was finished. I developed an overwhelming sense of inferiority.

The war came, with its appeals for workers, and I knew that two lives were being wasted within the confines of my home. My feeling of despair became all-consuming.

Then one day I read in my monthly Braille magazine a notice about guide dogs.

(Four months later Alfred Swede was at the training centre, learning to use the guide dog, Retter, that he had been given).

A year has passed since I brought Retter from the training centre and it has been one of the happiest periods of my life. Between us there is a complete partnership and I feel that we are bound by a common bond of devotion. I have taken a firm hold on life again. I am no longer a helpless human being, but a normal man with self-confidence and vitality.

The measure of my happiness is shown when I reflect that after four years of inactivity and hopelessness, now each day brings its fullness and purpose.

There was nothing I could do directly helpful to the war effort but I could now release my wife, who took up war work, and help other wives in vital occupations – by doing the shopping for them all. Retter and I knew where all the shops were situated and we soon became very well known.

People stop for a chat and I am glad, because not only is this conversation friendly, but it helps to bring about better understanding between the seeing and non-seeing communities.

A Free Man
by George Elder, who got his first guide dog, Gilda, in 1938.
"Would you like a guide dog, Mr. Elder?" I could hardly believe my ears.

For ten years I had been struggling along the streets with a stick, tapping the way in front of me and always straining my ears and nerves, expecting at every step to trip over a dustbin or a child's bicycle or kiddy-car that may have been left thoughtlessly by its owner.

For year I had suffered from dreadful headaches as a result of this strain; I could feel that I was getting old before my time, and was always worn out when I got home after being out, especially if I had been in a strange place.

When the Commissioner of the Girl Guides for Lanarkshire asked me if I would like a guide dog I did not hesitate to say that I would. I had heard of these dogs and had a vague idea how they worked, but I had never thought that I would have one of my own! The Girl Guides wanted to present one to me through the Guide Dogs for the Blind Association as their good turn for the Coronation, and I most gratefully accepted the offer.

I went to Wallasey a few months later to train with my dog Gilda. She was a fine Alsatian and I wondered how this dog, that I had never seen before, was going to take me through streets that I had never walked in my life before.

On my first morning out with Gilda I knew that here was the very thing that I needed to help me with my work as a poultry farmer and shop-keeper. No longer would I have to depend on my friends for getting about in strange places; I was free to go where I liked and just when I wanted to.

After two weeks' training I came home to Scotland with my new friend, and she at once settled down and made herself at home with the rest of the family. I soon discovered that new ways of earning my living were now opened to me; I was as good as any sighted man now, and could earn my living just as I had done while I was employed as an engineer at a coal mine.

For a year Gilda worked and played with me; she was so lovable in nature that it was a real pleasure to have her about the house: she would bring me my slippers, my cap, her harness and leash, and pick up her basket ready for the road. She took me through town, city and country without seeming to notice any difference. Traffic was nothing to her; she treated it with respect and always saw to it that I did not get in the way of it.

Then disaster befell poor Gilda; she had had an injury as a puppy and the trouble had lain quiet till she reached the age of two, when it attacked her. I tried everything possible to save her, but it was impossible.

One day I took her to see a vet who was attached to the veterinary college in Edinburgh, and as she was very lame I did not ask her to lead me, but took her on a leash.

When I reached the town I was quite lost, as I did not know the lay of the land. Gilda saw that I was in trouble. She turned round and took the leash in her mouth and pulled me along the footpath.

I could feel the tears running down my cheeks. Poor Gilda was more in need of help than I was, but she did not think so and was willing to work till the end.

After Gilda died I was in a terrible position. I had developed my business during the year I had had her and now that she was dead I could not carry it on. I really felt the loss of my dog more than I did the loss of my sight. I was like someone who had been deprived of sight with a sudden stroke, and could only find my way about with great strain and difficulty.

The Association at once offered me a dog to replace Gilda, but their funds were low and they could not train more than a few dogs at a time. I would have to wait before I could be suited with another.

During the period of waiting all the old troubles came crowding back on me. My headaches returned and the strained look came back into my face. The carefree feeling left me and once more I felt that I could not keep it up for long, but must surely be an old man before my time.

At last a suitable dog came along and once more I went to the training school, which by this time had acquired new premises at Leamington.

I could not be blamed for thinking that I could never get a dog to take Gilda's place; she had been more than a dog to me, and I felt that there could never be so kind and affectionate a friend as she had been.

I was quite wrong, as I was soon to find out, for Lena, my new dog, is just as devoted to me and to her work and is a popular favourite with all my friends and acquaintances. Once more I am a free man.

"Good luck and remember to take it easy for the first 50 miles."

✫ Chapter Three ✫

ADVENTURES WITH A GUIDE DOG

Even when the exhilaration of the early weeks with a new partner has gone, life with a guide dog is never dull.

As Fit as Folly

In 1931 Thomas ap Rhys became one of the first four people in Britain to use a guide dog. He remained a guide dog owner for the next 48 years and died in 1979 at the Bolton training centre where he had gone to receive his sixth dog. Among his many achievements, he was a champion race walker and in *The "Tail-Wagger" Magazine* in 1936 he declared that his training "was entirely due to Folly". Describing a race organised by St. Dunstan's, he wrote:

This five-mile walk was held round Regent's Park on November 16th [1935] – once round the outer circle and twice round the inner circle to make up the distance. Each competitor was escorted by an experienced race walker holding a tape about two yards long tied by a safety pin to the shoulder of the competitor's running vest. My escort was an athlete who had taken part in the September Brighton walk. The crack man amongst the totally blind competitors was Harry Boorman, of Peterborough, who invariably wins by a good margin. He improved his time this year by a minute and a half on last year's effort, but he only beat me by two seconds, so that I also beat his time of last year handsomely. My time was 44 mins. 32 secs.

Thomas ap Rhys was an outstanding competition walker and is seen here with Folly in 1939 training on Bangor pier.

I am very proud of the achievement because I was a raw novice at the game, and the only training I had had for the race was in walks with my guide dog Folly, an Alsatian provided by your committee. As the whole secret of race walking is in the proper swing of the arms, which I could not practice at all since I had to keep my left arm still at my side to hold Folly's harness, I can truthfully say that my training was entirely due to Folly. My training consisted of walking several miles every day – up and down the pier during the day, for that is pretty clear going during the winter, and then out on the road late at night when the roads were quiet, and I could walk as quickly as I liked without having to swerve past other people or wait at kerbs for the traffic to give me an opening. I think I am still improving and will do even better in the coming races. The next is a nine- mile walk – three times round the outer circle of Regent's Park – on January 18th.

★★★

"I am feeling as fit as a man can be," he wrote to Miss Muriel Crooke at the guide dog training centre in Wallasey, and shortly after reported on the nine-mile race.

Folly is very fit indeed. She is eating well, guiding well and really no trouble at all to me, but to the family – well, that's another story! My wife came up to London with me for the last race and the first night Folly was inconsolable. There never was a more affectionate dog, I do believe.

In this last race, nine miles, three times round Regent's Park, I won comfortably, lowered a long-standing record by a couple of minutes and, so a friend assures me, can now claim to be the world's champion blind walker! I was not content to train with Folly alone this time but got an experienced race-walker to coach me in style, of which I was up to then completely ignorant, and the man who beat me in the previous race by only two seconds, though he put up a very good performance, never really worried me this time.

Now for the 12-miles in a fortnight's time!

A Magnificent Mongrel

Sweep was a character, as Mike Tetley reported in the June 1986 issue of Forward.

Sweep was thought to be a cross between an Alsatian and a black and white collie. Friends said that he had a most unusual set of amber eyes that looked right into you. They frightened some people because he had an air about him that said, "I will do as I

am told but I will stand no nonsense".

He was kind to all animals and we often left him in the garden running free with the guinea pigs. He would look after them all day. He loved running and herding. If he was not herding the guinea pigs and my children brought friends into the garden, he looked upon them as his flock of sheep, keeping them together either by pushing them with his body or nibbling at their fingers.

Years later I was surprised to find out he used his body to clear a way for me through a crowd. On some occasions, when I was in a hurry to catch a train, if the way was blocked by a number of women talking and dawdling he would come up behind them, stick his nose between their legs, lift their skirts and blow. If this did not work he would put his shoulder against their knees and push them out of the way, making sure that my right shoulder never touched anybody.

I understand that most guide dog owners have a special rapport with their first dog because it is the first experience of regaining freedom of movement. I had that with Sweep. He had a fantastic word vocabulary. For instance, when I taught him to find the Piccadilly Line at St. Pancras, I sat him at the top of the steps leading to the Piccadilly Line and repeated the command. "Find the Piccadilly, find the Piccadilly, find the Piccadilly." Then he would hand me his paw. I never knew whether that meant, "I understand" or "Shut up". At St. Pancras I could ask him to find the Piccadilly or the Circle Line. Sometimes if I did not use the word Piccadilly for about six months he appeared to get a bit rusty and not move quite so confidently until I had reassured him.

In the same way, I had taught him to obey the commands "Find Boots", "Find the Post Office" and "Find the florist". When he was six we moved from Luton to St. Albans and in St. Albans I tried to teach him to "Find Boots". I could not. As far as he was concerned Boots was in Luton and you could not have Boots in St. Albans.

I thought another useful command would be to "Find a lavatory", particularly on a station. This was quite simple but on more that one occasion he took me to the women's side. I dropped

this command. Once when I was in a public lavatory I knew that Sweep must be popping so I said to him, "Come on boy, your turn, Get Busy". He moved straight forward, cocked a leg, aimed straight and stood back and indicated to me, "What next?". As I left the room I heard the attendant say

Mike Tetley and Sweep.

to the other patrons, "Did you see that dog?"

Maurice Hall (who had trained the dog) had told me that this dog would take me anywhere. I decided to put him to the test, so I set out to walk from Luton to London just with Sweep, a distance of 33 miles. We left Luton after lunch on a Saturday and covered the 11 miles to St. Albans in four hours. The A5, being a Roman road, was straight. I checked in at the Red Lion Hotel. During the walk Sweep made only one error. He took the left side of a Y junction but as the volume of traffic diminished I was able to correct the error.

The next day I did, however, ask for help to cross the A41 where it crossed the A5. It was very busy and not knowing the exact layout I was frightened. Sweep may have been able to do it but I did not give him the chance.

It took us eight hours to walk the last 22 miles to Marble Arch where we tried to check in at the Cumberland Hotel.

Two other long-distance walkers, George Cole and Ula, on the road from Land's End to John O'Groats in June 1985. The 69-year-old guide dog owner slept at night in a tent that he carried with other basic necessities on a specially-constructed trolley that he pulled behind him.

They would not let us stay there as it was their policy not to admit dogs, but they did put me up at the Rose Court Hotel, one of their subsidiaries. I had walked in shorts and thereafter every time I put on shorts Sweep thought he was in for a long walk.

Off duty, Sweep was the family dog. The children would dress him up. One day when I could not find him, I wandered round the house calling. In the kids' bedroom I eventually heard a flapping noise and on investigation found Sweep lying between the sheets with a bonnet on his head and a dress on ... he was the wolf in Red Riding Hood.

As Mr. Freeman said [see the next passage], he must have been brought up on a farm and had little knowledge of social behaviour. When he first came home we had to train him to be civilised. To my wife's horror she came in one day to find him sitting in the middle of her dining room table looking out of the window.

When I first got Sweep home he was an escape artist. Our garden had a fence six feet high. He jumped this. I put it up to seven and a half feet. He jumped this. Only when it was eight and a half feet and inclined inwards did we stop him. But not for long. I hope that no reader is so naive as to believe dogs cannot think. Sweep escaped over this fence because he had found a packing case in the garden measuring about four feet in every direction. This he pushed with his nose until it was about five feet from the fence. Then he ran back, turned, ran forward, jumped on the case and then over the fence. Just to make sure that this was not coincidence I moved the packing case. He then replaced the packing case and repeated his performance.

Thank you Sweep, wherever your spirit may be, for being my constant companion, my friend and my mentor to whom I poured out all my troubles in the early days of blindness. You always had your tail turned right over proving that you were a confident, carefree but magnificent mongrel.

★★★

Sweep was acquired in the early 1960s before the present breeding and puppy-walking programmes had developed. Derek Freeman described him as a dog that defied "everything that I believe in about early socialisation and exposure," and went on to say:

I got a phone call from a farmer in a village not far from Leamington. Apparently another farmer who had owned the dog had gone away and left him on the farm.

The farm was empty and the dog had been adopted by this other farmer at the opposite side of the road. As they had dogs of their own they didn't really require him but they didn't want to neglect him so took to feeding him for three or four weeks. They were getting a bit worried about him getting knocked down because he was a very confident dog and as there were tractors and other vehicles moving around the place, they left him tied up in an open Dutch barn most of the day. I said I doubted whether the dog would be any use to us, but at the time we were scratching around for anything really, so I said we'd go and have a look.

I remember going and looking at him and there was this dog of nice substance and character tied to a post supporting the Dutch barn. Now you could have expected a dog as big as him, and being as neglected, to be a bit protective about his pitch, but he wasn't. He welcomed everybody. I put him on a collar and lead, and as I couldn't assess him walking around the farm I took him. They didn't want him back in any case, so we could either use him or find a home for him. That also applied to the fleas he harboured. He had no owner, no home, no pedigree and no name.

He is one of the few dogs I've ever walked that exploded every myth about puppy-walked dogs. He'd never been off a farm, never been into town, never had any experience or education apart from farmyard language he'd picked up himself. I remember taking him up to the top of the Parade in Leamington. There are wide pavements to give him plenty of room. There were cars coming past and periodically he would stop and look at them and watch them go past. He didn't panic. If you could have ever said a dog had a human expression, that scruffy dog did.

As we went on I was talking to him and I remember a woman coming out of the butcher's shop at the end of the Parade with a pushchair. As he rounded the half-blind, the blind flapped and he just stood back from it. Then this jet-propelled pushchair came straight at him, enough to make a number of experienced dogs run. He just stood back from it. As the pushchair went past he smelt the scruffy kid in it and his tail was going like mad. I thought, Funny! It must smell familiar, (like a farmyard, I suppose). I showed him red buses on top of the Parade and he didn't panic at all as I stepped on and off the platform.

His expression at the things he was seeing was absolutely amazing. I took him in shops and as soon as he felt the slippery floor he hesitated, but with a bit of encouragement he got going. At first, it was if he was walking on hot cinders, not spread-eagled like a lot of dogs would at that experience. He was walking just as if the floor was hot, picking his feet up like a horse trotting.

Then he could hear people talking over the counter and he looked up, fascinated by it all. I wish we could have got it on camera. Then he was confronted by a big flight of steps. Well, I gather he'd never seen steps before; there was no way he knew how to tackle them. That was the first time I'd seen a bit of apprehension in him. He wanted to rush them but, after several attempts up and down, he got the measure of them.

He didn't know about travel because he hadn't done any. So we took him with us when we went out purchasing pups. He was a good traveller. He was good with cats. We also checked him on food. We took food from him and gave it back to him. In the end we looked upon this as a game.

The dog eventually qualified and I often wondered if his owner knew what limited experience that dog had before we got him. He'd been a farm dog and he blows to the wind everything that I believe in about early socialisation and exposure. I also think that he happens to be the one exception to the rule. He was a very sound dog, of good courage, willingness and correct sensitivity and you don't get many like him. Most dogs that came to us with that type of background are nervous wrecks, aggressive or protective.

Sweep was totally confident, totally serene, totally unflappable and of charming disposition. He made an excellent working dog despite his unfortunate start in life.

The Legendary Alfred Morgan

The first of the following passages conveys something of the qualities that made Alfred Morgan one of the more remarkable of the early guide dog owners. He was also a prolific writer – one of his articles is quoted in the previous chapter – and subsequent passages are a selection from his many vivid and moving accounts of the life that opened up for him after he acquired Bella in 1932.

On The Dot

From an article by Captain Alan Sington in The "Tail-wagger" *Magazine, January 1936.*

The last time I had seen Mr. Morgan was over a year ago, when, as it happened, both he and I went to a meeting of the North-Western Counties Association for the Blind at the Town Hall, Chester, which began at 2 pm. Mr. Morgan lives in Walton, from where he travels daily to Liverpool, where he works at the Docks.

Alfred Morgan acquired his first guide dog, Bella, in 1932, the year after the first four guide dog owners were trained in Britain. He is seen here giving a demonstration for MPs in Parliament Square in 1936.

He went as usual that morning to his work, leaving the Docks about noon, in time to catch the various connections (consisting I believe, of the Overhead Railway and the Mersey Ferry) to take the train from Birkenhead, arriving at Chester Station at 1.40. From there he had a mile or so to walk to the Town Hall, where he said he would arrive in time for the meeting. He had not been to Chester for years – not since he lost his sight – and his dog had never been there before. Someone at the meeting said he could not arrive in time, but Mr. Morgan walked in at five minutes to two! He also had an appointment at Wallasey that evening and went there from Chester, having to go to Liverpool and out again, later returning home via Liverpool. That day, he and his dog, Bella, alone together, travelled 62 miles, using three trains, two electric trains, four boats and walking seven miles, and kept the two appointments to the minute.

Where To?

From a report by Alfred Morgan written about 1935/6.

When it was said in an article some three years ago that I had only to whisper in Bella's ear and tell her where I wanted to go and she would take me, I was quite annoyed at the time, for it really was nonsense and made me feel such a fool. However, I am afraid that I have to admit that that very statement is absolutely and literally true to-day. I talk to Bella a great deal in an ordinary conversational tone, and just as though she were a human and could understand. I have a great habit of saying to her when we are in the train together going home of an evening, "I say, Bel, I think we'll go and see Ginger after dinner," or it may be Effie, or George, or anyone of our many friends. She is generally sitting on the carriage seat by my side when these conversations take place, having forty winks, but she raises her head, looks at me, pokes me with her paw to say "Right-ho, bo," and promptly goes to sleep again.

When we get home we go through our usual routine. I first of all have my dinner while Bella sits patiently on her rug under the table, but she knows that immediately I have had mine she will have hers. After she has had her dinner, instead of settling down for a snooze as she usually does, she keeps very much awake and watches me like a cat watching a mouse. At the slightest move I make she is up and after me and if I am reading or listening to the wireless, she gets impatient and begins poking me to hurry me up. When we do get up, she makes straight for the place I have mentioned, whichever it may be.

You may remember that last December we had a long spell of very bad fog, the worst we have had for years. All those three years the trains had never let me down. But on the worst of these foggy nights last December, they did. I arrived at Lime Street to find all traffic stopped; nearly all street traffic had ceased also. The few trams crawling painfully along were absolutely packed and you could walk twice as fast. I never waste time in an emergency like that. It is about three and half miles from our house to Lime Street Station. I turned out of the station along Lime Street, up London Road, down Norton Street, up Islington, on to Shaw Street, that is, where we struck our old route of three years ago.

So far I had had to give Bella her orders, which was easy, for I knew exactly where I was, but from then on she took charge. She knew exactly where to go though it isn't what you could call an easy way, being all steps:– you know, right, left, right, left, all the time. She even crossed over the road going down Beacon Lane, because on that side was a long sidewalk running along the Convent Wall without any "ups and downs" in it. And it was both dark and foggy. We arrived home at 6.45, half an hour after our usual time, when we have the advantage of the train, and five minutes before the time we arrive on the many occasions when we miss our first train through the dock bridges being off and so delaying us.

A Rum Affair
From an undated letter to Miss Crooke written in 1934/5.
Three men were walking the same way as ourselves, smoking and talking. They were walking very slowly indeed and Bella stalked after them. She will not go into the road to pass people if she can help it, and I do not make her do it, as it might prove dangerous some time if she did so in town. So we followed slowly after them, until Bella found an opportunity of passing. When this sort of thing happens I generally say something to Bella to attract their attention, such as "Come along Bella, get a move on," which generally has the desired effect, and they turned round, or at least one or two of them did, for they spoke to Bella, but they didn't let us pass and we had to follow a little further, but our chance came

at last. The pavement was rather narrow and they were apparently straggling across it, for Bella kept dodging from one side to the other in her efforts to pass. However very soon they must have closed in a little for she walked quickly to the side of the pavement and got past them. When she does this kind of thing, her tail goes round with a mighty swish, carrying me around with it, and with another swish in the opposite direction, we get into the straight again. People tell me that it is quite amusing to see us in a busy street, executing "horse–shoe" bends and "S" curves through the crowds, and you must remember that I do not touch a single person during this performance. However, on this occasion we slid past as usual, and one man who had apparently not noticed us before, said, "Gad, that's a fine animal." "Yes," said another, "I have been watching it. It's been following us for some time." Then the first said, "That's a rum affair on its back. What's it for, I haven't seen one before." All this happened in a flash as we were sliding past them, and I was now in the middle of the pavement about two yards in front of them. I knew by the way they spoke that they had no idea what was the matter, so I did what I am beginning to do rather often lately in similar circumstances. I held Bella back firmly, so as to walk slowly, and put out my stick to gently touch the wall which I knew was close by, then I said to Bella, "Up you get, Old Girl," and away we went. It was a very slight action, but it was enough. They must have tumbled to it immediately, for I heard them say in astonishment, "Lord, he's blind! That thing's to guide him." "It must be the chap who was in the paper, he lives somewhere about here." But Bella and I were off.

Coping With The Raids
From a letter to Miss Crooke, 18 December 1941.
Here is a point I would like to shout out all over the country. I am

speaking of Liverpool, but it applies to everywhere. Do you realise that of all the blind people in Liverpool, only FOUR are going about, and have been going about, in their usual normal way. Those who are not evacuated are now handicapped worse than ever by the loss of many of their "landmarks" by the raids. The FOUR, of course, are Miss James, Miss Johnson, Miss Evans, and myself. Our problem isn't landmarks, but obstacles. And they are not really difficulties, they are merely disconcerting when one comes on them suddenly. The dog does the rest.

Re-routed

From an article entitled 'My War Dog', published in the February 1942 issue of The "Tail-Wagger" Magazine. *Morgan called Fly his war dog because he brought her home on 2 September 1939, the day before war was declared, and because "it is really the war, or rather the air raids, which have brought out her best qualities". Describing a situation caused by the bombing and a traffic jam, he continued:*

When the jam occurred, she stopped, gave a swift glance at both blocked corners and the now blocked roadway, looked at the waiting line of vehicles alongside which we were passing (on the offside, in the road), turned on her tail and walked back a few vehicles to where there was a small space, and so gained the pavement. The way was still blocked in front of us, so she hesitated a second, and then deliberately went down a small side street and then along another at right angles, and rejoined our usual route about 200 yards further down. I knew exactly what she was doing, for I remembered these streets but had never been along them, and I did not check her.

A large number of people had watched the performance, and some who were walking my way, were not slow in voicing their amazement at the way in which Fly had handled the situation. One man put it rather tritely, if somewhat bluntly, when he said, "She made a … of a sight better job of it than most of us would have done," and I agree. It was no question of routine. She was suddenly faced with something quite out of the ordinary, and I am certain she knew exactly what she was doing. In other words, I am convinced that she thought the problem out to its logical conclusion.

Loud Applause

From a letter to Miss Crooke, 30 January 1942.

This is the third snowy winter I have had with Fly, and she is really marvellous. Snow must be her natural element. I am not joking about this, but I am firmly convinced that of all the people tramping up and down to the docks during last week, I was probably the least inconvenienced. In the big open spaces on the docks, and in the steep streets leading down to them, the gusts of wind had piled the snow in deep drifts. I was told of these things, of course, but I didn't experience them, for Fly chose the easiest way. Of course, I found myself doing the strangest things,  crossing and re-crossing the road at unexpected places, but I let her have her own way, and then would be told by someone why we did it, much to my amusement. One of her little tricks caused not only amusement but great admiration for her acumen among the dockers and others who noticed it. You will remember that when you go on the Dock Estate from the Dock Road, you go through gates with policemen guarding them. It is just under the

Overhead Railway, and when it is raining crowds of men stand there sheltering. By the way, people who work on the Docks call the Overhead "The Umbrella" because they walk underneath it when it is raining. Well, Hill Street, which we come down towards the docks, is not quite opposite our gate, so we walk a short distance along the Dock Road, along a pavement, of course. But when the snow was on, the pavement was deep with snow, while under the Overhead was comparatively clear, so "Cutey" did something she had never done before; she walked along the railway lines under the Overhead, to the loud and profane applause of the onlookers. You know, the general public still have a very hazy idea of the work of guide dogs.

"My man's a bit off colour, I'm taking him to the vet."

A Tragic Accident

The two letters that follow were written by Miss Crooke to Captain Liakhoff on 4 and 7 of September 1942.

Morgan has had a very serious accident. He is in the Royal Southern Hospital, at Fazakerley [near Aintree]. He has had both thighs broken and an arm. He has had a blood transfusion but is not expected to live.

Miss James rang up to tell me this evening when I was out and left messages with my Father. Sir Lionel also rang me up later. I do not know if anyone has let you know so am writing now. From what I can gather he was coming down Hill Street – evidently on his way to work and evidently this morning – he hesitated in the road and a lorry came right into him. Miss James said that witnesses say that it was not the dog's fault. Sir Lionel believes too that it was not. Fly is alright and with the people that Morgan lived with.

More Hope

I went to see him in hospital yesterday, and his condition is slightly improved.

Most unfortunately, however, one of his legs must be amputated. He is conscious, doesn't feel any definite pain, and doesn't realise the seriousness of his position.

I spoke to the doctor and he said that, although at first they did not expect Morgan to live, there is now much more hope.

As far as I can find out up to the present, the accident happened in this way: Morgan was crossing the street not at the corner, but some distance from it and just at the side of a large stationary car. There was, therefore, no view of the street from his right until this car had been passed. The lorry was travelling straight, but very fast. Morgan's landlord, who was at the scene of the accident very soon after it occurred, spoke to some people who had actually witnessed it. He told me that these people said that they saw, very distinctly, how the dog tried to pull him back when she saw the lorry.

Morgan Bounces Back

Two letters from Alfred Morgan, who was still in hospital, to Miss Crooke, dated 14 January and 21 March 1943.
Well, here I am at last with a real live letter of my own. What a relief it is to be able to carry on one's own correspondence.

I was going down Hill Street to work, and had just reached the usual spot where I cross the road to the old Southern Hospital. As I crossed Grafton Street, a cross street, I heard a horse wagon coming along it. It was a very noisy affair, and I think it misled me somewhat. Fly stepped to the edge of the pavement and looked up and down as usual, and began to cross the street at her usual quick pace. Just as I stepped off the pavement the horse wagon arriving at the corner stopped, and in the comparative silence I heard a motor coming down the hill at a good pace. It was moving very quietly, probably under free engine as the street is quite steep. I knew it was fairly close, but it didn't worry me and Fly kept steadily on and I knew that I was halfway across the road ...

Before I had taken two more paces I felt him flash past behind me. Fly was struggling to get me along but I held her. As I felt the thing go past I let go the harness and she sprang onto the pavement out of danger, but only just in time. The back of the lorry skidded and the back wheel got me ...

I came to about 10 minutes later in the casualty station to find the doctor picking out my top denture which had been smashed to little pieces in the fray ... All this time there was a terrific row going on in the waiting room next door. Fly was dashing about the waiting room and taking running jumps at the

door to the room in which I was, trying to burst it open. They said they could do nothing with her, and asked me what they could do. I told them to wipe her feet and legs with a damp cloth and bring her in. The nurse immediately went out and two or three minutes later came back with Fly. She was inclined to be a bit boisterous at first, but when I put my hand on her head she sat down and licked my hand until one of the boys came some 10 minutes later. Fortunately it was one of her special pals, or I don't know what would have happened. After a bit of fuss she consented to go quietly and I haven't seen her since …

The wheel went over both legs about four inches above the knee. The right one was badly damaged, the left one a clean break. They put the left one in a Thomas splint, but I was so bad they could not touch the right one for some days. I had blood transfusions and forced feeding and all that. At the end of six days they simply had to do something, so off it came …

On December 29 I was measured for an artificial leg. It is expected to come along by the end of Feb. My left leg is my worst trouble at the moment. The 16 weeks in the splint made it stiff at the knee, ankle and foot …

And now, what will be the end of all this fuss and bother? My own idea is very definite indeed; but whether I can carry it out or not is quite another matter. Quite a number of Job's Comforters are already telling me that it is impossible, but we will see about that. My idea, of course, is to go back to the Yard, and to have a dog again; Fly, if possible, but if not, then a slower one … I must have a dog; if I can't the whole arrangement will collapse as far as I am concerned.

Learning to Walk

I have been here 28 weeks last Thursday; quite long enough, thank you. I have been measured and fitted for my leg, that is, I have had it on in a rough state, and it had to go back to be finished off ... I had it on for well over half an hour, and did a lot of walking on it. It did feel queer, but not half as bad as I imagined it would. I quite understand now what they mean when they say I will have to learn to walk.

Another Dog
Letter from Captain Liakhoff to Miss Crooke, 26 August 1943.
Thank you very much for your letter and your most helpful letter about Morgan ... My plans about him are as follows: I have prepared a dog (a small crossbred Alsatian bitch) very gentle and not pulling hard. In the meantime Forbes' dog died. (You will remember him, I think you trained him with Lady.) His way of walking is somehow awkward, as he has something wrong with his legs, and this has increased since he had his first dog. In order to give Morgan's dog a real experience I thought I would give her to Forbes temporarily and see how he gets on. A month or two before Morgan comes I will take the dog back, will try it and adjust anything that is necessary.

Forbes' opinion of the dog is very high indeed and I think that this experience will facilitate Morgan's training with the dog. I did not tell Forbes for whom I wanted the dog, but just said that it was for someone more unfortunate than he, who on top of blindness had an artificial leg. The old man was very nice about it, and said that he would do anything he could and would give the dog back with the greatest of pleasure knowing that he was helping someone else.

The Great Adventure
Letter from Alfred Morgan to Miss Crooke, 4 October 1943.
Well, here I am, ready for the great adventure. In other words I'm going to Leamington on Thursday morning ... I have improved

wonderfully since I saw you at Orleans House some five weeks or so ago. About a week after that Miss Bartlett, the lady who is in charge of the Massage Dept. at the hospital, came to me and said we were going to finish with the actual massage, and would concentrate on balance. So she put me in charge of an energetic and extremely lively massage student, who leads me about the place on the end of a strap ... they put chairs and stools and rolled-up mats and pieces of wood all over the floor, and I have to follow the girl around quickly dodging around the stools and stepping over the obstacles. Of course, I'll never meet anything like it in the streets, but if I can manage them without toppling over, following a nice respectable guide dog will be like eating pie. In fact, I'm preparing to have an argument with Capt. L. He tells me that Betty, the new dog, walks nice and quietly without any pull on the harness, but I'm afraid I will want her to pull quite a lot. It will help to steady me ...

By the way, have I told you about Fly? When they took me into the casualty station at the old Southern Hospital one of the nurses had to keep Fly quiet. They got on so well together that when the nurse changed her duty and came to our ward some months later and probably thinking, like so many other people, that I would not be able to make use of Fly again, she asked me if I wanted to find a home for Fly, to give her to her mother for company. About three months ago Capt. L told me point blank that I wouldn't be able to use Fly again, so I told Nurse Green that she could have Fly. So about two months ago Fly went. They live just outside Southport ... It's a champion place for a dog ... they are all very happy and comfortable together.

On the Loose
From Another Pair of Eyes, *by Peter Ireson, published in 1991.*
At the end of the year Morgan went to Leamington to collect his

new dog, Betty. But no sooner had he returned to Liverpool with his new guide than more trouble struck: someone left open the door of the house in which Morgan lodged and Betty slipped out. All that day he and his landlady, Mrs. Hartley, searched the neighbourhood, but the dog had vanished. The next day the headmaster of the local school allowed him to enlist the help of the two top classes and 60 or 70 boys joined the hunt.

"The boys were far more useful than the police," Morgan reported. "They told me all about her movements and tried to get her, but unfortunately they thought of it as a round-up and when they got her cornered, made a grab at her, and off she went."

It was six days before a policeman called Morgan and Mrs. Hartley to a field in which he had spotted Betty. They walked up and down calling her name and the dog soon emerged from some bushes.

"She stood and looked at us for a moment, and then ran towards us. But there was a great 6ft barrier of barbed wire between us, and she couldn't get through. Then she ran along the wire towards the gate. It is quite a large field, quite a quarter of a mile in length. The policeman saw her coming and made to keep her in the field, but she got scared and leapt over a high wall into the road. Mrs. H left me standing in the field and gave chase. People and children kept her on the track and at last, after chasing up several streets, she found her crouching down in a corner. She called her quietly and Betty ran up to her. Mrs. H was so excited that she couldn't put on the harness or the leash, which she had, but picked her up and carried her back to the taxi, and when Betty saw me she simply flew at me, shrieking with joy. The rest was easy."

Six days on the loose had apparently done the bitch no harm. But she had escaped just as she was coming into season and returned pregnant. Liakhoff's advice was to have the pups put down at birth but Morgan was all for keeping two or three of them, for Betty's sake, even if it meant losing her as a guide for some weeks. It appears that he did send Betty somewhere to have her pups, but there is no record of what happened afterwards. In any event, she cannot have lasted long as a guide dog because Nora Robinson, who in 1944 married a Russian serving with Czech forces in Britain, remembers training a dog for Morgan in 1945, when she returned to work after having a baby. "She was a wonderful bitch. When they got to the pavement he would put his head right down to the dog's ear and say 'Forward'; and they would shoot across the road. He wasn't a very tall man, so he didn't have far to stoop. We couldn't get him to stand up and say 'Forward'."

[Morgan's adventures are recounted at some length, not because he was unique, although he was certainly a remarkable man, but because he demonstrated in striking fashion the determination possessed by so many blind people, a quality without which they can never realise the full potential of a guide dog. His story is an eloquent reminder not only of the joy that guide dogs have brought to so many lives, but also of the courage and perseverance that are needed to enjoy the fruits of this remarkable partnership between man and dog.

Alfred Morgan was elected an honorary life member of The Guide Dogs for the Blind Association in December 1944. He died in 1966.]

Bess Knew What To Do

One of the four guide dog owners that Alfred Morgan observed were the only blind people able to move around Liverpool freely once the air raids started was Margaret James. She was a masseuse at Liverpool Royal Infirmary, where her guide dog was affectionately known as

Margaret James and 'Sister Bess'.

"Sister" Bess. In the November 1945 issue of Forward, *she wrote the following account of how Bess helped her to get to work every day through the wreckage left by the raids.* As everyone knows, Liverpool had its share of the blitz. The hospital is in the heart of the city, and I live some two and a half miles away, and nearly every raid brought some new difficulty by bomb damage along the route. Roads would be blocked, tram routes cut. If I had had to depend on myself and the trams, I could not have carried on. But I had Bess. She knew what to do. For instance, we might be walking along one of our usual streets when she would suddenly cross the street and continue on the other side for some little distance, and then re-cross and go on as usual. I knew that some building was down and the pavement blocked, and would make enquiries as to the best way to proceed. This sort of thing happened many, many times, but it did not hinder me from arriving at the hospital. The hospital itself was hit on more than one occasion, but the work kept on just the same. On the first occasion I arrived as usual and turned down the corridor towards my department. The place seemed strangely silent; none of the usual bustle and clatter of patients; and the floor was covered with fine grit. Before I realised what had happened – we had only taken half-a-dozen steps into the place – Bess stopped and stood looking for a brief moment, then turned and walked me out again. The corridor was blocked with debris. We went in by another entrance and found our department intact.

When I look back at those months of horror I wonder how I managed to do it, but at the time it seemed the normal thing to do. The fact is, I couldn't have done it if it had not been for Bess.

Misguided

One of the classic guide dog jokes is about the blind person who stops someone to ask the way. The sighted person then bends down and gives instructions to the guide dog. Tony Castleton, who is now the Association's national fund-raising manager, once had an experience that was not all that different.

I can remember coming down by train from Kings Lynn to Liverpool Street and talking to a man for some time. He asked lots of questions about guide dogs.

When the train arrived at the station he asked if he could help me. I said," Yes please. Perhaps I could meet you on the platform." I harnessed Marco up, took the overnight bag down and went to the door of the compartment. Bearing in mind all the questions he had asked, I thought he was quite knowledgeable about guide dogs, but I will never forget what he said. He said, "I am over here chum, I'll take your dog if you can manage your bag."

Life-Saver
William H. Binning in Forward, *1956.*
To return to Sally – on two occasions there is no doubt she saved me from serious, perhaps fatal, injury. The first was on a zebra crossing on a main road near my home. I was half-way across when a fast-moving car failed to stop, and without hesitation Sally swerved and stood firmly in front of me, preventing me from taking another step. I only felt the "swish" of the offending car as it raced by. Some onlookers saw what had happened and applauded her wonderful presence of mind and prompt action. The second occasion was when I was preparing to alight from a train at Brockenhurst. We went out of the compartment to the corridor. I opened the carriage door and gave her the command Forward! She resolutely refused to move. I then realised that the familiar platform noises were coming from the other side of the train, and that Sally had prevented me from falling onto the railway line.

Goosed by a Guide Dog
From the Letters column of Forward, *March 1989.*
Sir, It was a hot day in Cambridge. I had received a formal invitation to attend a reunion dinner at my old College. Slightly apprehensive, I had accepted, and had indicated that I would be bringing Ian, my German Shepherd, with me – this despite strict regulations forbidding dogs in College. Indeed, Byron, so the story goes, kept a bear in his rooms instead of a dog!

A friend had driven me to Cambridge, and was to spend the night in lodgings and then drive me home again on the following day. Having installed me and Ian in our rooms in College, we set out to find the lodgings.

The pavements were crowded, the traffic heavy. As we passed St. John's College, we encountered a log-jam of pedestrians.

Roger Elgood and Ian.

Now, Ian likes to step it out, and was anxious to find out where we were going. I could feel him looking round the inside of the obstruction – no room there, and round the outside – too much heavy traffic to do an off-kerb there, thanks very much, and so we had to wait.

But not for long. After a few seconds there was a sound between a gasp and a squeal, the log-jam parted, and we sailed majestically through. I spoke over my shoulder to my friend. "What was that all about?" The reply was swift and abrupt. "Shut up and keep going." Somewhat mystified, I complied.

Fifty yards later, we were able to stop and I demanded an explanation.

Apparently the log-jam had been caused by a lady of ample, not to say voluminous, proportions who, with her diminutive husband, was completely blocking the pavement. There was no way round. Finally, Ian had taken the law into his own hands, and pushed his long, wet and extremely cold nose up the back of her skirt. That shifted her!

As we passed by I understand I received a very dirty look

from the diminutive husband. Did he think I did it, I wondered!

F.R.H. ELGOOD, *Saltburn-on-Sea, Cleveland*

The Other Woman

Being "the other woman" in the life of a guide dog owner inspired Mrs. G. Pitman of Jersey to share her experience with readers of the 1959 edition of Forward.

My husband had spent a month in her company before he decided to bring her into our home. She was a ravishing brunette with the most wonderful brown eyes and her vital statistics were such that you would not have bothered to give Marilyn Monroe a second glance if she were around. Even I had to admit that she was attractive. The neighbours raised their eyebrows and declared in hushed whispers over the garden fences that they had never seen the like before and I suddenly found that I had been supplanted overnight and that the household now revolved around her. As she endeavoured to explain to me, I must now realise that I had, to a certain extent, to take second place and that henceforth she would be my husband's constant companion. And so I became a slave to the "other woman" in my husband's life. His main concern was for her. Had I remembered to get the little delicacies that she liked so much; had I seen to her every comfort. If I wanted to go to the cinema my husband would explain patiently that she did not like films and we could not possibly ask her to remain at home. If we were invited out I had to ask if our hosts minded if she came too and at times I could almost hear eyebrows being raised at the other end of the telephone. She and my husband go up to town to the office together each day and return together at night. If by any chance my husband goes out and leaves us both at home, she will wait with one eye on the clock and fling herself into his arms the moment he comes home. Before her entrance into our lives, my husband and I used to sit together on the settee in front of the fire each evening but now, oh dear, no! She apparently wouldn't like that arrangement, so I have been banished to the armchair on the other side of the fireplace while he shares the settee with her.

She has been in our home for nearly three years now, and I have become more or less reconciled to it all. However, I have felt these last few days that I must tell someone about it and having written it all down I feel a lot better. But listen, I hear footsteps – it's my husband and – oh yes, she is with him. How could I expect it to be otherwise. The sitting-room door opens and there she is. She pauses and gazes at me and – whoosh – everything is scattered to the four winds as 65 lbs of boxer guide dog hurtles itself into my lap in rapturous welcome and licks me furiously.

Settling In

Another wife who wrote in Forward *(1950) about life with her husband's guide dog was Mary Jones.*

In the beginning my husband and I thought of the dog very much as a means to this one end, independence of movement for him: he being active and energetic felt very keenly the necessity of being dependent on anyone, even a wife, for his comings and goings. We were considerate for each other, and for that very reason were often in the position when neither of us would express our real feeling for fear of worrying or disappointing the other. I think this is a situation which must inevitably arise and which imposes a strain upon both parties, however closely united they may be. When my husband first went into "open" employment, our difficulty was a very real and practical one, for I was in a job as well, and our working hours did not always coincide. From time to time we were able to make arrangement for an escort but they were never satisfactory for long, and were often a source of worry. (I must in fairness to other people say that this was during the war when everyone had many and varied claims on his or her time). I remember now, when my husband first had his dog, people would say to me, "Aren't you afraid to let him go?" The answer was that from the first I found it far less worrying to see him step off with the dog than to put him on a bus and wonder if Mr. X would turn up to meet him at the other end.

So I am primarily grateful to the dog for relieving me from this anxiety and freeing much of my time and energy for other purposes. I have been able to take a new job, one very much to my heart, which I could not possibly have managed in our pre-guide dog days.

If, however, I am to describe my own feelings really frankly, I must digress here to say that I did not find the "change over" entirely easy. Looking back now, I realise that it needed considerable adjustment on my part as well as my husband's, before we finally settled into a new way of life. My husband naturally was very much engrossed in his new experiences to the temporary exclusion of other things in which we had been mutually interested. Moreover, I could see that for a time his energies were concentrated on working out problems in which I could not share. I felt very much of an onlooker in those early days and it is not easy to remain an onlooker when you are accustomed to going in with offers of help, however much you realise the rightness of the position.

But this was only a transition stage and though it was strange and sometimes difficult I found it tremendously interesting to see him start off, like an explorer, on new journeys and to listen to his reports when he came in. I shall always remember my real thrill of pride and excitement the first time that by chance I met my husband in the street; he was coming towards me through the shopping crowds just like anyone else's husband. As for the dog himself, I was ready to love him from the start but was held back by the thought that I must not interfere; in course of time this problem was solved by the dog himself, who indicated that he was prepared to accept me as quite a desirable appendage to my husband. Now there is a real bond of affection between Mick and myself. I never interfere with his work, or his discipline, and he is pre-eminently my husband's dog, but he obviously regards me as part of the home-life, someone who ought to be about!

In fact I realise now how many of our early queries were settled by the dog himself; at first we thought of him as a separate entity, a strange new factor introduced into our home – we had not reckoned on the warm, living personality of the dog, loving and lovable, and we had not the experience to foresee that he would become, as he is now, an essential part of our home-life.

I am aware, too, of another change in our married life, one that affects my husband primarily but has its natural reaction on me. It is rather difficult to formulate this in words, but I will try. I know that blind people vary very much in their attitude to the sighted world. My husband was always one of those who tried to "keep their end up"; he liked to join in conversations with sighted people on an equal basis and to this end often drew on my experiences which I had related to him, and my descriptions of things that I had seen. Since he has had his dog he lives very much

more through his own experiences than through mine, because he is able to find out things for himself and can join in purely masculine activities, such as Toc H, if he wants to do so, and that is why I say that life is fuller for both of us, not only for him. We have more to give to each other because we are both free to follow our own lines of interest.

Prudence Falls Ill

From Eyes at My Feet, *by Jessie Hickford (1973).*

It was only when Prudence was seven and a half years old that a shock came. The end of a normal day came, and as far as I knew a perfectly healthy Prudence curled up on her bed and went to sleep. I retired upstairs. During the night I was awakened by some sound or other and was immediately alerted to listen for Prudence. Perhaps she wants to go out, I thought. I heard her reach the bottom of the stairs where she appeared to stumble. It seemed to my listening ears that she came up the stairs awkwardly, stumbling again. I was on my feet in an instant, in an anxious frame of mind, before she had entered the bedroom. I quickly put on my slippers but did not stay for a dressing-gown. Before I reached the door, I felt her nose touch me, and then she turned to lead the way out. I followed slowly, talking to her as I went. At the head of the stairs she stumbled and then, to my horror, I heard her falling body slither down the stairs and reach the bottom with a thump. "Oh Prudence!" I cried involuntarily, and tried to hurry down the stairs. I wondered what I would find. To my amazement and relief, I heard Prudence move; I put out my hand to feel her. She was on her feet and moving very slowly along the hall towards the back door. As I opened the door she collapsed at my feet and lay motionless across the doorstep. She was crumpled up in such an unnatural position that I feared she had died. She must, I thought, have felt desperately ill when she came up to me for help.

Jessie Hickford and Prudence.

Now this. What could I do?

I was alone in the house and near to tears. I felt my watch and found that the time was just after four o'clock. Should I wake the neighbours? But what could they do if she were dead, came the awful thought. I knelt down and laid her more comfortably on her side. I felt for her heart-beat but could not feel it. Then I thought I caught a faint sound and listened intently. I was sure then that I heard her try to swallow. I touched her body again, and felt the slightest response in her legs. Thank God, she was at least alive. All this takes time to tell, but in reality it had happened very quickly. As she lay motionless, I sat on the floor beside her, pondering what to do. When I realised how cold I was and that the door was standing wide open, I thought of a cup of tea. Action of any kind was welcome, so I shut the door and slipped on a coat which was hanging in the hall. As I set about making a cup of tea, my mind was playing round the problem: what, if Prudence had had a heart attack, could I give her?

By the time the kettle split the silence of the night with its shrill whistle, I had the answer. A spoonful of honey in lukewarm tea could help if only she would drink it. I touched her again; there was no answering movement, but my straining ears caught the sound of swallowing. I placed the saucer of tea and honey close to her nose on the floor. Then, oh joy, I felt her try to raise her head. Supporting her head in one hand I pushed the saucer under her nose with the other. Scarcely moving, she drank a little and stopped. I put away the saucer and laid her head down gently. She lay quite still.

I then began to drink my cup of tea, and before I had finished it, Prudence rose to her feet and walked, oh so slowly, into the dining-room. There she sank on to the floor under the table and lay stretched full-out motionless again. I knelt by her, stroking her head and talking to her. She made no response, but

I knew that she was alive and warm. Apart from whatever it was that had caused her to fall she must also be suffering from shock. Warmth and rest were therefore essential. I left her lying there on the warm carpet and went upstairs to dress. It was still not yet five o'clock when I was dressed and sitting in the armchair waiting for dawn. Then, and only then, did I realise fully what this accident to Prudence might mean to me. If she had heart trouble, even if she recovered from the fall, she could not continue to work as a guide dog. I resolved to keep her whatever happened. I simply could not let her go as a pet into someone else's household. If she really had heart trouble then she could not continue as a guide dog. At that moment I did not consider going to retrain with a new guide dog. All my thoughts were on Prudence. I sat thinking of all the things she did for me and how lost I would be without her bell. In the meantime Prudence lay still and the whole silent house seemed to be listening and waiting.

At half past six I breakfasted and gave a saucer of warm milk and honey to Prudence. This time she raised her head without any assistance from me and lapped the milk strongly. She moved only her head to drink and then lay still. Over an hour went by and then she moved. She rose to her feet and moved slowly to her bed in the corner of the room. She clambered on to it and curled up. So far, so good, I thought.

As soon as I could reasonably telephone the veterinary surgeon, I did so. He said that he would come as soon as he could. After he had arrived and had given her a thorough examination, he confessed that he was puzzled. Her heart action was irregular and could have caused the faint, but there were no other signs of deterioration. He advised me not to work her for the time being and left tablets to help her heart action. He called again the next day, and by then Prudence seemed considerably better. By the end of a fortnight, after several very careful check-ups, she seemed quite fit. The cause of the fall remained a mystery, but a few weeks later I had reason to believe that I had found the answer.

Prudence had been lying flat out on the floor, after a long run in Friday Woods, and when she rose to her feet to greet a friend her right leg gave way and she stumbled. She stumbled again as she moved forward. Later during the same day her leg gave way once more. Her foot was not injured and the leg did not hurt her so I tried to remember anything that could have strained or jarred the leg muscle. We had been taken out in an old car that had a back seat that was high off the ground, and I wondered if it was just too high for a seven-year-old dog to jump from. Perhaps, I thought, she landed awkwardly and twisted her foot slightly. I also wondered whether a weakness in the leg had caused her to lose her footing on the stairs the night she fell. I thought it likely then that what she had suffered from had been shock and concussion. At any rate, I resolved there and then that, in future, whenever she was ready to jump from the back seat of the car I would hold her by the collar so that I took some of her weight as she reached the ground. Since that day this is what I have done, and I have not noticed any further weakness in the leg.

✶ Chapter Four ✶

PUPPY TALES
AND STUDENT DAYS

From 1931, when guide dog training started in Britain, until well into the 1960s, the training centres picked up potential guide dogs wherever they could find them – with the inevitable outcome. Three-quarters of the dogs taken in for assessment were rejected as unsuitable and even those selected for training were likely to be a good deal more difficult to handle than today's specially bred and reared dogs.

The full story of the dog supply problems of the early days and the rise of the breeding and puppy-walking schemes from the late 1950s is told in *Another Pair of Eyes*, published in 1991, and a short extract from that book sets the scene for the passages that follow. The people who care for the Association's breeding stock, and who endure anxious days and nights during the whelping and early weeks of the puppies' lives, provide a voluntary service without which it would be almost impossible to supply the training centres with the high-quality dogs that are needed today. The same must be said of the hundreds of puppy-walkers who raise the potential guide dogs in their homes from the age of six weeks to the time they are ready to start their training at about a year old. Their tales of wrecked gardens, ruined furniture and homes destroyed by a succession of juvenile delinquents display a tolerance and good humour – but, above all, a devotion – that must surely secure them a place among the saints.

A Mixed Bunch

From Another Pair of Eyes, *by Peter Ireson (1991).*

For 30 years or more the training centres obtained their dogs from farms, dog dealers, breeding establishments of varying quality, and a host of other uncertain sources. It was like trying to build a racing car out of bits of scrap metal. The dogs were neither bred nor reared for their highly-specialised and demanding work and it is remarkable that they succeeded as well as they did.

Those selected for training were a very small proportion of the total number taken in for assessment. Some would be rejected almost immediately. There are heart-rending accounts of training staff going down to the railway station to collect dogs that were in a dreadful state: mangy, half- starved or dying from distemper. Others would die later during one of the periodic outbreaks of

"Have you got one that doesn't walk so fast?"

disease in the kennels. As time went on the isolation of new intakes of dogs and the use of vaccines became more common, but as long as large numbers of "approval" stock were arriving from uncontrolled sources there was always a health risk.

Collecting the dogs when they arrived at the local station also presented another risk – to the training staff. The dogs would be chained inside the guard's van and many of them, particularly those inclined to be nervous or apprehensive, would be extremely aggressive by the time they arrived. They were supposed to be wearing muzzles, but sometimes they managed to get them off. Arthur Phillipson remembers one dog that ate its muzzle; all that was left was the end of the strap.

Many of Leamington's dogs arrived on a train that was scheduled to stop at nearby Milverton station for one minute, and on many occasions a long delay was only avoided by unhooking the guard's van and leaving it in a siding while an unfortunate trainer patiently calmed the dog so that he could release it without losing his hand. One technique was for the trainer to lie on his stomach, which the dog would recognise as a submissive posture, and gradually creep forward, talking all the time.

"You had to watch its reactions," Arthur Phillipson recalled. "Sometimes it would take an hour or more. On a winter's night, after a hard day, we used to curse the telephone when it rang just after 11 o'clock and a voice said, 'Milverton station here. We've got a dog for you'. When we got the dog off, we had to take it down to the kennels, prepare bedding, feed and water it, give it some exercise – by then it was well after midnight. Of course, coming in like that set all the other dogs off and the barking would disturb the neighbours."

Many of Bolton's dogs arrived on trains that were going through to Manchester and Steve Lambert, who joined the centre as an apprentice in 1964 and is now regional controller for the North West, also has vivid memories of dealing with half-crazed animals in guards' vans that had to be left in a siding. Bolton staff would often use a dog-catcher – a loop on the end of a long pole – and on one occasion were even driven to throwing the dog a piece of meat doped with a tranquilliser in order to calm it down.

The assessment period for these "approval" dogs lasted up to three weeks, by which time 70 or 80 per cent would have been rejected, largely for reasons of temperament, such as nervousness, aggression or sound-shyness. Disposing of the large number of rejects took up a good deal of valuable time. Some would be returned to the senders, but often this was not possible, and the reason for rejecting the dog could make finding a home for it difficult. The Association's reputation suffered, too, because people would take a reject thinking the dog would be all right in their loving home, and then blame the training centre when the dog was still being anti-social some months later. They usually failed to recognise that the dog's behaviour was a product of its earlier background.

The dogs that emerged successfully from the selection process were still a pretty mixed bunch: generally tough and streetwise, often of uncertain age and nearly always badly behaved in one way or another. It was quite common for them to be cat-chasers. Derek Carver, a former director of training who became an apprentice in 1954, remembers seeing a working guide dog take off after a cat that it had spotted, dragging its bewildered owner over a low wall and halfway through a hedge before it gave up the chase.

"That sort of thing was quite common," he observed. "But the owners were expected to deal with it and they regarded it as a bit of a laugh. It was assumed that dogs would chase cats."

Nevertheless, there were some remarkable individuals

among them. John Weeks trained a German shepherd that was much quicker at learning than most: "I remember going out with her and coming across a branch that was perhaps 14 feet long. The dog went over to it and looked up at me and I said, 'All right, go on then'. The branch was quite thick at one end, tapering off at the other. She didn't try to drag it away. She picked it up and, half releasing it from her mouth, worked her way along until she found the point of perfect balance. Then she walked off with maybe four feet sticking out of one side of her mouth and ten feet out of the other.

"I used to play a game with her where I threw a ball into a bucket of water and she would pick it out. On one occasion I threw a ball that sank to the bottom. This puzzled her for a bit, but when she spotted it she put her paw in the bucket and found she could move the ball. The next bit sounds incredible, but I swear it happened. She stirred the water with her front leg until the ball came to the surface and she was able to snatch it out with her mouth."

Some of the dogs are remembered for being "characters" as much as for any outstanding abilities. Arthur Phillipson trained

'Soon we were taking everything in our stride...'

a beautiful rough collie called Baron which went to a Mr. Jones. While Jones and Baron were out training one day in Leamington, under Phillipson's eye, they stopped at a kerb beside a shop in which there was a Yorkshire terrier.

"He was a nasty little devil," Phillipson recalls. "On this occasion he flew out of the doorway and growled at Baron, who was sitting quietly at the kerb. Baron just picked him up by the scruff of the neck, Jones gave the command Forward, and they set off across the road with the terrier getting a good shaking as they went!"

After Baron released his persecutor, the little dog ran off squealing with his tail between his legs. "Serves him right," said his owner, the shop-keeper, when Phillipson hurried across. "He's always doing that." Jones, meanwhile, carried on quite unaware of the adventure in which his guide dog had been involved.

On another occasion Phillipson was out supervising three students who were working their dogs around the town. One of them, a young woman, had a golden retriever who was tempted by a pheasant that was lying on the open slab in front of a fishmonger and game dealer's shop. As the dog walked past, and without pausing, it took the pheasant in its mouth and carried on, tail wagging and pleased as Punch with itself. Again, the dog's owner was not aware of what had happened until Phillipson spotted them and intervened in order to return the pheasant.

One of his more unusual trainees was an "approval" dog called Patch that was probably a cross between a greyhound and a whippet. It was given to the Reverend Glyn Thomas, who was very strict chapel and a teetotaller. The dog's previous owner obviously wasn't, however, because one morning Thomas and his guide disappeared while out on a training walk and were eventually found sitting at a table in a pub. It was a summer's day, the bar had just been cleaned and the doors left open, so the dog decided to take its owner in. Realising he was lost, but not where he was, the minister sat down, waiting to be rescued. He was horrified when he discovered how his guide had led him astray.

Despite this inauspicious start, Thomas and Patch settled down well together. The story has a sad ending, however, because Patch was killed one Christmas in a quiet little Welsh village where Thomas had gone to stay with a friend. He'd let his dog out for a run, after being assured that it was quite safe because there was never any traffic. Unfortunately, on that occasion there was just one motorcyclist who came racing down the lane and hit Patch.

The First Six Weeks

Mrs. Doreen Hart's two brood bitches, Amber and Liz, once had litters on the same day. With 22 puppies and three cats to feed, she was soon

Doreen Hart

producing 100 meals a day. Mrs. Hart *wrote about one of Liz's litters in the June 1980 issue of* Forward.

Liz gave us very little warning at all. She even ate her tea, which is most unusual before the big event.

It had been a lovely day and we had been for quite a long walk in the morning, though of course she couldn't keep up with Amber in rabbit chasing and climbing steep banks. I was blackberry picking and she helped, if that is the right word: both she and Amber are expert pickers but the trouble is they both eat all they pick. And they choose the big juicy ones.

We came home and Liz inspected all her nest sites in the garden and did a bit more digging. In the afternoon she had her usual sunbathe and then her tea. Her puppies were not due for a few days and she wasn't really very big.

During the early evening BBC news and weather forecast I noticed she was panting and couldn't settle. I went with her when she asked to go out and she did another inspection of all the nests. I said to her, "Look, if you're having them tonight, you'll have them in your box in the kitchen," and in we came.

The whelping box had been ready for the past week with plenty of newspapers handy and a cloth over the top to keep out the light and make it a little private. Also the small box where I put the first ones born whilst she attends to the newest arrivals. Just in case it was to be that night I put a hot water bottle under the blanket in this. There was a furious tearing of paper as Liz was preparing the best nest yet. Her mother, Amber, cleared off – she believes in keeping a very low profile during other people's confinements.

Then two or three pushes, a bit of a cry – there was the first puppy: a little dog. Liz adores her puppies and while I usually break the membranes when they are over their mouths, she competently manages everything else. The very vigorous washing and licking the bitch gives them stimulates the pups and, in a motion rather like a seal on dry land, they find a teat and start to suckle. This is when you breathe your first sigh of relief.

Well, another whelping had started, and the first puppy looked fit and healthy. Ten minutes later the second came, this time a bitch, so Guide Dogs will be pleased! Liz was busy cleaning up and washing them and the first puppy was noisily objecting to being denied its drink. The next four puppies were born at 45 minute intervals and the first-born was already dry, with pale yellow fur feeling like warm silk.

There was a pause, but I was sure there was another puppy to come, as Liz seemed very restless. So I gave her a drink and persuaded her to come round the garden, where she paid a call. The glow-worms and the stars provided all the light we needed. We came back in and I settled her with her babies and sat back to wait.

I always feel there is something very special about the relationship between my dogs and myself at this time: it's as though they know they can manage, but how good it is to have someone on hand just in case.

Liz got up and moved round the box, crying a little, so I quickly moved the puppies to my small box in case she trod on one of them. One or two hard pushes, a bit painful, and the last puppy, a big girl, arrived. Her family was complete: four bitches and three dogs. Small by Labrador standards, but it would not make excessive demands on her. Liz is an exceptionally good mother and this was her fifth litter.

I put clean paper in the box, gave her another drink and settled the puppies with her, making sure the last-born was suckling. Determined to see the sunrise, I let up the kitchen blind. There, shining through the trees was the Morning Star, Venus. Soon the distant mountains were visible, then the sky flushed pink and the light grew until I could see the sheep in the fields surrounding us.

Liz and the puppies were all fast asleep. I took a walk round the garden, drank a cup of tea on the kitchen step and then took one up to my husband. Next I fed Amber, and my three rather-put-out cats. Liz was watching – she loves to see what is going on, so her whelping box is not made too private. I gave her a drink of milk.

Full House for Christmas
by Mrs. Gillian Cree, in Forward, *March 1982.*

On 30 November we had two dogs in the house: our own two yellow Labrador brood bitches, Kree and her daughter Questa. By Christmas we had 15. The big addition came on 1 December when Questa had her second litter, giving birth to 12 beautiful puppies, seven dogs and five bitches.

Gillian Cree with Gill, Gina, Gem, Grace, Gretal, Guinness, Garry, Giles, George, Guy, Gus and Grant, when aged two weeks.

Initially the puppies thrived, but by the third day it became obvious that Questa was unable to produce the amount of milk required and was beginning to look weary. So on the advice of our vet I began to help her out by feeding six puppies every two hours. I swapped them over each time, so that they all had an equal share of being with mum. The six puppies not with Questa I kept warm in a box by the fire and at this point Kree, their grandmother, took a keen interest in them.

Kree is an experienced brood bitch, having had seven litters of her own. Indeed, her last puppies had left her only two weeks before. I decided to see what would happen if I gave her the six puppies away from Questa to care for and she took to them immediately, licking them and fussing them, and they contentedly snuggled up to her.

There was just one problem. Kree wanted the whelping box for this. After all, she knew that was the right place. But Questa was rightfully already installed in it, and things began to get difficult. My husband quickly solved this problem by knocking up some timber to make a second box and the two bitches settled down well, one each side of the conservatory.

We still had to keep up the two-hourly feeding programme, of course, because Kree did everything else for them except feed them. We were pleased that she didn't start producing milk again, so soon after her own super litter, as she is now eight years old and it would have pulled her down.

This went on until the puppies were four weeks old and in addition to the two-hourly feeding ten times a day, I had to get up at the ghastly hour of 3a.m. to change the six puppies over from grandmother to mother as they were by this hour desperate for food. After those four weeks the puppies, Kree and Questa were all doing well but I was myself very weary!

In the midst of all this came Christmas and the arrival of my friend with her guide dog, bringing the canine population up to 15, plus two elderly cats. This meant that on Christmas Day food was prepared and served for 98 animal meals plus those for seven adults and two children, making it a Christmas that will not be forgotten for many years.

As I write this the Christmas festivities are over. The puppies are five weeks old and I can see a light at the end of the tunnel – but unsuspecting puppy walkers will soon have a G litter descending on them. Soon, too, the cats will be able to sleep undisturbed by the fire; I shall be able to walk around without a trail of puppies following me; my husband will be back at work; the children will be back at school; and my friend, with her guide dog, will have gone home.

What on earth shall I do with my time?

●●●●●●●●●●●●●●●●●●●●●●●●●●●●●●●●●●●●●●

A Missing Eyelash

It was recognised in the 1930s that dogs raised in the right conditions would be more likely to succeed as guide dogs than those that had grown up without any special conditioning. Several attempts were made to start puppy-walking programmes, but it was not until Callum McLean, a member of the Association's Council, came on the scene in the late 1950s that a rearing programme was developed successfully. His drive and leadership ensured the growth of the work, and he was soon being helped by Ted Harte, another member of the Council. When McLean moved to Scotland in 1964, Marjorie Woolmer joined Ted Harte in supervising the scheme and she wrote in the 1969 issue of Forward about her experience of puppy-walking.

"May I talk to your puppy?" asked the salesgirl who sat at my feet in the shoe shop one busy Friday afternoon last autumn. "Certainly, please do. She's very friendly," I replied rather absent-mindedly as I tried to decide which of several pairs of shoes would best see me through a winter of pavement-trotting which is the lot of all concerned with the production of guide dogs.

Katie, the nine-month-old Alsatian sitting so demurely by my side, was overjoyed at being noticed and responded instantly by extending a long red tongue towards the girl's face. Then there was a scream of dismay which caused everyone, assistants and customers alike, to stop dead in their tracks. My salesgirl had her hands over her face. "This is it," I thought, "Katie's nipped her nose and I shall be accused of keeping a dangerous dog." Visions of a court case rose before my eyes. "What on earth's the matter?" I asked her, a little irritably perhaps because I don't like people screaming at my dogs. "My eyelashes," she wailed, "she's swallowed my eyelashes!" She lifted her face from her hands and, sure enough, one eye had a thick, black fringe of false eyelash, and the other was as nature had intended it to be.

"Open your mouth at once," I said to Katie, suppressing an

instinctive desire to laugh and trying to look suitably stern and disapproving. Katie sat there with an expression of exaggerated innocence on her face which might well have fooled anyone who did not know her as well as I did; she was enjoying being the centre of attraction. Obediently she opened her mouth and, sure enough, there on her tongue lay the missing eyelashes in a demure semicircle, looking little the worse for wear. I picked them off, and returned them to their owner. "I'm insured against this sort of thing," I said, "would you like me to buy you another pair?" "Oh no, it's quite all right," she replied and to the huge delight of a shop full of fascinated onlookers, she stuck them back on again ...

How often have I watched the kind, patient faces of the trained guide dogs as they go about their work and thought to myself, "If only their owners knew what they used to be like!"

"Chris was a wonderful dog," says her trainer to me with a faraway look in his eyes. He still remembers her with affection though it must be at least five years since he trained her, and goodness knows how many dogs have passed through his hands since then. I'm sure he's right and I'm very glad it is so, but my chief memory of her is of having to watch helplessly as she hurtled over the churchyard wall in pursuit of a squirrel just as a funeral procession left the church door to wind its way down the path to the graveyard. It started out slowly and reverently enough but as Chris wove in and out of the band of mourners, round and round the gravestones, intent only on the fleeing squirrel, order and decorum were largely abandoned. "Always welcome your dog when it returns to you", advise the books on dog training. "Do not let your puppy chase moving objects," warns the *Guide for Puppy-walkers*. I wonder if the authors of these admirable books were ever so sorely tried as I was at the moment when Chris eventually returned to me, in her own good time, knowing full well, I am convinced, that in view of the solemnity of the occasion, I was unable to administer the correction she so richly deserved …

I wonder if Maggie's owner ever takes her down to the pub for a drink? From his photograph he looks a jolly sort of chap who might well spend some time in the local, almost certainly with Maggie for company; but I can recall an occasion when Maggie, then aged about four months, and her elderly stable companion, sat side by side in front of a bar while a stout, motherly body hung yearningly over them. "Aren't they gorgeous," she gushed. I watched the puppy's eyes as they followed the swing of a pendant hanging from a thin gold chain above her head. "She looks like someone watching Wimbledon," I thought. I should have been quicker off the mark for without ever getting up or shifting her position, there was a little snap and the pendant had gone.

I have learned, with the passage of time and a number of such mishaps, to be very wary of telling people that I'm walking a guide dog puppy. No, I only admit it if they are behaving exceptionally well, for one must consider the reputation of the Association. My puppies are well known in the village. "Swallowed any good eyelashes lately," they call as we pass by, and the Vicar knows better than to include us in the annual service of blessing the animals, although we obviously stand in need of it!

The Character of Finham
by Kate McCutchion, in Forward, *August 1983.*
Can you tell me why a Labrador puppy would find a compost heap such an interesting place? Easy. There's food there. Maybe we think it is rotten, but to Russel it was clearly delicious. It was unbelievable that such a lovely-looking animal should have such a disgusting habit.

There was the day he stripped the washing off the line, dragged the Persil-white sheets down the length of the garden and rolled on them. So he had to be taught to leave the washing alone.

"No she's not yet housebroken but the house is."

When he felt it was time to venture further afield he decided to climb (yes, climb) the fence and trot round to see the butcher. Oh no, not to steal anything, just to check the sirloin was in its right place. The butcher brought him home. There was no doubt that Russel was becoming the character of Finham, where we live, near Coventry.

I think he is part lion and only part Labrador, but they say not. He could knock a defenceless Granny off the dining room chair and then walk over her. His size was enough to make everyone wary, but the power behind him even at that age was just incredible.

His greatest love was to play with his friend Sam, a black Labrador. Ten minutes together and they were exhausted and ready for a drink and a sleep. Sam was a great factor in Russel's training. Without Sam he would not have enjoyed his freedom so much. An older dog who loved to run and play was just what Russel needed, for the older dog could teach him much.

Unless provoked to do so, Russel never barked at home, but in kennels he barked a lot.

When he was good he was very good but when he was naughty he was horrid. Like the time he ate the wholemeal chocolate cake, straight from the oven. Not a crumb was left and there was no dog to be seen when the deed was discovered.

He would be on top of the compost heap, unperturbed, and when Bill went to look for him his tail would wag enthusiastically on seeing his master.

Or the day he decided to pick all the roses – every prize bloom.

The worst experience came a week before he was due to leave us. I was in the kitchen when I heard a loud bang. Immediately I ran outside to see if Russel had jumped over the fence and into the road at the side of the garden. I called and there was no response – I could see neither hide nor hair of him in the road and likewise drew a blank after scouring the garden. My two boys and I got into the car and drove round the area. Still no sign of Russel. We called at Sam's house but he had not been there.

By this time we were very concerned, so I informed the police and advised the puppy-walking centre. We sat and wondered where he could be when suddenly Alistair and Philip, who had both been walking round the garden, rushed in to say they had found Russel. He had trapped himself in the cold frame. While busy gathering Bill's geraniums the lid had closed on him, squashing him down. True to form he just lay there and made himself comfortable. The police laughed heartily.

Right to the end he was the life and soul of the party.

Simple as it was to criticise some of his activities, he had the most adorable nature. He could not get close enough to you. He was exceptionally good at returning to his bed when told and would stay there, willing the daily raw egg to come off the plate and to his mouth, but it never would. When told he was a good boy he could have it, he was out like a shot.

Are all puppies the same? Mischievous and adorable? One thing is certain: the love and trust between a man and his dog is everlasting and I know that Russel as a guide dog will love his master and give him as much pleasure as we have had. He will be older and more staid then and have had more training. I wish them both many years of happiness and mutual trust together.

Never again!
by Joan Laidler, in Forward, *December 1985.*

Puppy walkers must be a strange breed of people. We voluntarily have our lives turned upside down and expect to shed tears when the little darlings leave us – having meanwhile shed others through sheer frustration when we had them.

We puppy-walked a couple of years back and had the most horrid little pup called Estelle, a yellow Labrador. I did not think it was possible for anything so beautiful to be so naughty. She was a real rebel in every sense. Just when I was beginning to get some response from her, half way through her training, I was taken ill and had to go into hospital, so Estelle went elsewhere to finish her training. We heard she eventually qualified.

I have owned, bred and trained dogs for over 20 years. Currently our family owns a three-and-a half year old golden retriever and a two-and-a half year old rough collie, Emma and Heidi. They are beautiful, placid and obedient.

Once I was back home and had picked up after the illness I suggested we get another guide dog pup, but my husband and children said, "No. After the last one, never again."

My two "girls" both had litters and without Estelle life was happy, quiet and enjoyable – was, until Zillah arrived. You see, after a family discussion we decided in spite of everything to apply again.

Zillah arrived: a tiny, ugly scrap of noise and energy. You name it, she did it. She bullied our dogs, screamed at night, destroyed everything from house plants to the kitchen sink. Her leash-training was awful. She decided she would not walk on any lead if she could possibly prevent it; when we did get her on a lead she pulled hard over to the right. She picked up everything from sweet papers to half bricks. She dived at other dogs, people and prams. As we walked down the street she grabbed garden plants. She watched traffic with an evil look in her eye.

One good thing about her; she was house-trained within five days.

Although she was so naughty I felt it was due to her great mental and physical ability, and believed we would be able to overcome the problems.

Another good thing: Zillah was desperate to please. Unlike Estelle, she tried to be good but found it hard not to be naughty. I knew there was a great deal of hard work to be done before she was trained, but if the first little devil had made the grade, then surely we could achieve success with this one.

People thought we were mad. "Send her back," they said, as though she were damaged goods to be returned to the shop. We looked upon her as a challenge – and soon as a member of the family, albeit only for one year. She was to be someone's eyes for many years and even on bad days, when she reduced me to tears, I would not think of sending her away. She was affectionate and felt bad about upsetting me. We love her and she loves us. For all her faults she is a pleasure to know.

She soon learned the word No, and what was and what was not allowed. Although she is still destructive, she is not as bad as she was. She no longer bullies our two "girls". She now walks well on the lead and around shops, without nicking the goodies off shelves. She is quiet when left alone, and responds off the lead. She ignores people and other dogs.

Zillah can still have her naughty days. After one of these our 13-year-old son said, "Mam, can you remember what life was like before Zillah?"

"Yes, Craig," I replied. "Very boring."

Demolition Job

The vandal that caused all the damage in this story was not an up-and-coming guide dog. Brig was a pet that belonged to guide dog owner Miss Elaine Blair and she wrote about him in the September 1986 issue of Forward *in recognition of the puppy-walkers who had raised guide dogs for her and thousands of other blind people.*

Way back we got Brig, our pet long-haired black and gold Alsatian, as an eight week old pup. We read all the appropriate training manuals and were determined to turn this ball of fluff into a veritable saint.

Until he was inoculated, Brig had to use newspapers in the house when needing to answer the call of nature. He learned this lesson so well that we had problems changing this habit when we were able to take him to the park after his series of injections. I clearly remember one day walking the pup for miles and showing him acres of luscious grass to perform on. But Brig waddled home, immediately used the newspaper, and was as pleased as punch at having managed to hold out so long.

Thereafter we had to take newspaper with us and lay it on

the grass until he got the idea that he could do it without the paper.

I also remember one earlier evening when he had proudly dragged the *Radio Times* along the lounge carpet to my feet, performed on it, and then wagged his tail in glee because he thought he had been so good and done right.

As everyone knows, puppies vary in their degree of activity in chewing anything vaguely chewable. One day I entered the lounge to find Brig sprawled along the hearth rug with a torn plastic dustbin liner at his feet, gaily eating teabags, potato peelings and much else. Brig's demolition list was a daily occurrence; he devoured his plastic bed and a plastic vegetable rack, not to mention 3lb of potatoes, a pound of carrots, a pound of onions, a leek, a cauliflower and a cabbage. I recall a day when I felt his stomach to see if I could locate my last wooden spoon being slowly digested, and on another occasion to see if there was any evidence of my three vanished houseplants plus their pots and soil being processed in his cast-iron stomach.

"You should have started in here!"

Then there was the day I walked into the kitchen to find he had dug up two layers of lino, stripped the newly-put-up wallpaper and dug a sizeable hole in the plaster, leaving white powder all over the place. He chewed through our electric blanket twice, literally ate jumpers, and chewed slippers for breakfast. Even the vet was amazed when Brig managed to chew his way out of a kennel and through a door into the reception area.

But do not despair, puppy walkers! Lots of courage and limitless patience prevail to win the day. We now have a big cuddly teddy bear, so well behaved you would never believe this passive lump was the same horror who demolished our last home.

Hard work pays off in the end. So good luck and many thanks to all puppy walkers. We GDOs are more grateful for the hard and often trying work you do, not once, but time and again.

Raiding the Fridge
From Puppytails, *a newsletter for puppy-walkers in the Midlands, December 1986.*
Never underestimate the strength of a Labrador's nose.

Labradors' noses may be soft and wet, but they are also extremely strong. My first puppy, Vaughan, was getting fatter and fatter – the Vet told me off, Maureen threatened to take him into kennels for some hard slimming – but we just couldn't understand it. He was having tiny meals, no biscuits, still the pounds rolled on. Just before he burst, I caught him opening the fridge door, having whatever he fancied and shutting the door again. We just hadn't realised he would have the power in his nose as there's a pretty strong suction on the fridge door. With a houseful of teenagers and their friends, I hadn't realised they were not responsible for the missing food. I kept a chair in front of the door afterwards and Vaughan became a normal size again.

My second dog, Taylor, wasn't into fridges, but windows! Fortunately, after opening them he showed no signs of getting out, he just used to hang his head out and accept the praises of his public passing by. We had to put a stop to his window opening in the kitchen at night. He might just as well have hung out a "Welcome Burglars" sign!

Ivan hasn't yet demonstrated the power in his nose – perhaps because he is only 75% Labrador.

Putting a Foot in it
by Sheila Martel in Pawse, *the newsletter for puppy-walkers in the South East, Summer 1990.*

Ida was such a good puppy. As a first time puppy walker, I marvelled at how GDBA could breed and select such well-behaved puppies. "Just you wait," said my experienced puppy walker friend, Estrid.

The months went by, and Ida grew into a gentle, sensitive and obedient dog. Her only rebellion was an occasional attack of cloth-ears and a slight sulk if reprimanded. She was clean day and night from nine weeks old. "Just you wait for the next puppy," said Estrid.

Then, one warm summer night when Ida was about eight months old, I was woken by a whimper at the foot of the stairs. Stark naked, I jumped out of bed and went down the pine staircase in the dark. Half way down I smelt trouble, and on the next step, I was in it. My foot shot from under me, and I landed on my back at the bottom of the stairs. There was "sh ....., you know what" everywhere! – between my toes, up the wall, and all down my badly bruised back.

I lay there for a minute, hoping that the crash would not wake my young male student lodgers, and imagining the sight that would greet them if they came to investigate – one plump naked landlady lying with her feet in the air, in an odour of anything but sanctity.

First things first – let the dog out, back upstairs for a dressing gown, hobbling on my heels trying not to spread it any further. Half an hour later I had washed the walls, my back, the stairs, and soaked my feet, helped of course by Ida who was feeling much relieved, and thought this was a good new game. I finally carried the bowl of grotty water through to the kitchen, caught my sleeve on the door handle, and shot the lot all over the floor!

Ida was such a good little girl! Several months later, when I was battling with Thomas – rumbustious, defiant, wicked, irrepressible and totally adorable, I knew what Estrid meant.

[When, at about a year old, the puppies have grown into young adults they exchange domesticity for the more communal and purposeful life of a training centre. There are fewer "characters" nowadays among the recruits than there used to be when they came from less privileged backgrounds. But ... dogs will be dogs! Some of their more memorable qualities and exploits are recalled here by training staff and the blind owners they went on to serve as guides and companions.]

Making the Right Decisions
Mike Csernovits on how a guide dog uses its initiative.
One woman that I trained at Exeter left the training centre with her dog at the end of the week and had to return to work the following Monday before I was able to visit her and go over routes with her. When I did get to her home in south London in the middle of the following week I accompanied her on her journey to work. We had to take a surface train first to Victoria and she'd been shown the way to the station by her husband, who was partially-sighted. So that was no problem. When we arrived at Victoria I said, "I'll have to follow you because I don't know where I'm going."

"That's no problem," she said.

Now, the dog had never been to London and the woman

was totally blind. They had been taken once across Victoria station to the Underground by the woman's partially-sighted husband, and here they were undertaking a none-too-easy journey to work without any difficulty. That's initiative. A dog lacking in initiative could never have done that.

Another guide dog owner told me that one day when she was out with her dog she was getting pretty fed up because it kept walking in the road and would not take her back up on the pavement. After a while someone who had been watching them came up to her and said, "I thought I should tell you that your dog will not go back to the kerb because there's a sheet of ice like glass on it."

That's initiative as well.

I also remember a case where a dog tried to use its initiative but was prevented from doing so by its stubborn owner. At that time it was common for coal to be delivered loose and dumped on

"You were right and I was wrong!"

the footpath, and on the day that I turned up on an aftercare visit there was a very large pile of coal just outside her house. I expected the dog to go "off kerb" to get them round the pile, but when it attempted to do so its owner administered a sharp correction and told it to go straight on. The dog still tried to go round and got another correction for its pains. It even tried a third time to take the sensible course but when it received an even bigger correction it gave up and led its foolish owner on an undignified scramble over the top of the pile.

The Last Trump

Steve Lambert, who is regional controller for the North West, will never forget the incident of the toy trumpet, or the guide dog that could never quite reconcile himself to retirement.

I was re-training this big, black woolly dog – one of the old "approval" stock of unknown parentage – that had been a guide dog for about six years. Its owner had lost a leg, but the dog was still trotting along at a normal pace and the man couldn't keep up with it on his artificial leg. We'd brought the dog back to the training centre to be slowed down and I was out with it in Bolton. I was waiting at a crossroads beside a pram in which there was a child with a toy bugle. The mum was talking to someone and not looking at the child.

Well, the child blew the bugle straight into the dog's right ear. The dog just shook its head. The mother told her child not to do it again, but as soon as she turned away to resume her conversation the child gave the dog another blast of the trumpet. It was about to do it for the third time when the dog quietly put its mouth round the end of the bugle and nipped the end of it together. That was the end of the noise ...

Shep was a collie who travelled every day with his owner, Frank Hoyle, to the workshops where Frank was employed in Wigan. They would take a bus to the bus station in town and transfer to another bus for the second leg. Shep did this journey year after year until the time came for him to retire.

Well, Shep had a winter of retirement by the fire but, come spring, he started to get restless. One day Frank went off to work with his new dog and during the morning Mrs. Hoyle, as usual, let Shep out into the garden. But this time he disappeared. An hour later he turned up at the workshops.

After that, every now and again, he'd go and sit at the bus stop, at the front of the queue, get on the bus and sit under the stairs, then transfer to the second bus at the station and continue on to the workshops. He did that right up to the final few months of his life. Nobody knew when he was going to do it. Sometimes he'd do it for four days running, and then maybe he'd just go on the odd day.

The Perfect Guide Dog

Neil Ewart, who is now the breeding manager, remembers training an outstanding product of the breeding programme, a male yellow Labrador called Ivor.

Training him was a doddle, and he went to a piano tuner in Hertfordshire. He worked for 11 years without ever making a mistake and, for me, he was the perfect guide dog. One of the routes his owner used was a little footpath alongside a railway line. It was quite narrow, and in the half-light one day the dog suddenly stopped and would not go on. His owner discovered that a fishing line had been laid across the path. I thought at first that Ivor must have touched it, but it had stopped some distance short. How it saw the nylon line in that light I just don't know.

I once trained a young man who'd lost his sight in a fall from

BLIND PIANIST OF THE YEAR

some scaffolding. He'd been given up for dead and although he did survive, he suffered some brain damage as well. But he had a wonderful sense of humour. One day he disappeared while out on a training walk and when he eventually turned up I discovered that when he got to a kerb he told his dog to go on instead of turning left. Well, as it happened, a double-decker bus had stopped right in front of them and so the dog stepped onto the platform followed by its owner. The bus promptly drove off.

The man was quite unperturbed by the incident. "I told him to go on, and he got on. That's alright, isn't it?"

One of the first dogs I trained was a Labrador – a wonderful dog but, my God, she was greedy! We had to feed her away from the rest of the pack. You'd put her food bowl down and she'd take down a pound and a half in one gulp. The blind person she went to had never had a dog before and when he first fed her – I'll never forget his reaction – he just said "Bloody Hell!".

Another dog ate all the food from bowls that had been prepared for all the dogs. There must have been 30 pounds of meat there. It just keeled over and we had to get the vet to it.

The Pig

Paul Holden, who was a trainer in the late 1940s and early 1950s, remembers two labradors.

Everybody who has had a Labrador knows what pigs they are. Raja was also an accomplished jumper. In the morning the kennel maids would take the food down to the kennels while the dogs were in the runs. Raja was in the run that day and heard the bowls going down. The kennel maid went to do something else and while she was away Raja jumped over a six-foot fence from one run to another, then over into a corridor, then over a barn door to where the food was. He quickly worked his way down the line of bowls and polished off 12 full-sized dinners before the girl returned. He was blown up like a balloon. Suddenly, there was a great burp and it all came back. But before she could stop him he gulped it back down again.

It was two days before I could get the harness round him again.

"We finally found the right dog for you."

The other Labrador was one of a pair of enormous puppies of about six months old that we had been given. I think it was called Major. I have the fondest memories of that dog. It took to the work like a duck to water. I'd given the dog to an enormous Yorkshireman called Patterson who was not only blind but also half deaf. It had tremendous enthusiasm and seemed to sense that this big lumbering Yorkshireman was absolutely dependent on him and his care. I have a picture taken just after the dog has stopped at a kerb and braced itself because it knows that its owner is going to continue past it. Another picture shows the man walking straight towards a lamp post with the dog doing its best to pull him round it.

Anyway, he had complete faith in this dog and the dog obviously responded.

To Hell and Back

Brian Moody, who retired as director of operations in 1992, talks about the importance of the rapport between a guide dog and its owner.

A dog will go to hell and back with a good handler. If you've got a really good handler there's no limit to what a dog can achieve. But nowadays fewer people think about their responsibility for bringing out the best in the dog. They want instant mobility. Blind people are no different from anyone else, of course, and we all want more for less. But the dogs have sometimes got to be angels to cope with it – they've got to work despite their owner.

I remember training a dog for a man who had had a stroke and couldn't speak. He had such a feeling for animals that he overcame all communication problems and they worked wonderfully together.

There was a woman I trained with a big male collie. They were a perfect team. During training I tried to trick them by arranging the obstacle course in confusing ways, but they never put a foot wrong. Unfortunately, the dog had to be withdrawn after about four years. She lived in a very run-down home in Birmingham with a layabout husband and a pack of kids and the dog just went to pieces. She seldom used it and it roamed the streets, but it was a wonderful dog and in her prime she was a very sympathetic handler.

Making a Good Match

Creating the right partnership between man and dog is vital if the long programme of breeding, rearing and training is to reach a successful conclusion. The person who lacks confidence can be helped to some extent by being given a dog with plenty of self-confidence and initiative. The dog has to be very carefully selected, however. A confident dog probably needs firm control, something the hesitant individual may not be able to give adequately. This can lead to the dog taking advantage of its owner. On the other hand a dominating handler with a dog of low initiative could inhibit it to such an extent that it stopped taking decisions.

This balance between a dog's need for control and an individual's ability to provide it is one of the key factors in matching dog and blind person. Training staff usually get it right, but Bob Steele, who is the senior training manager, remembers one occasion when they didn't.

This was an experienced guide dog owner who needed a replacement. He ran his own business and had a number of men working for him building sheds and garages. His previous dog hadn't worked out well and I promised him that he would succeed this time. I gave him a golden retriever that was well above average ability and quite sensitive. But he just couldn't handle the dog. He criticised the dog for having no initiative, but the problem was that he had such a strong personality that he totally inhibited the dog. It was a complete mismatch.

The dog was subsequently re-trained with a woman and it worked really well for her. She was a gentle, sensitive woman and very considerate with her dog.

There are sometimes sad situations when we try very hard to help someone but it just isn't possible. There was one young man of 22 or 23 that I desperately wanted to help. He'd been a relief manager at MacFisheries in Wakefield. One day after his girlfriend had thrown him over he went out, had a bit too much

"Well! Which one do you fancy?"

to drink, I suppose, and then fell down the stairs when he got home that night. He had a cardiac arrest and, although he survived, his brain was damaged.

He applied for a guide dog – he was desperate for one – and we did everything we could for him. But his thought processes were so slow. You would tell him something and you could almost hear the penny dropping. The whole training centre wanted him to succeed, but he didn't.

Sometimes we can help a person who is deaf as well as blind. There was someone in Scotland a few years ago, but he had a useful degree of residual vision. More recently we've trained a profoundly deaf girl in Peterborough. She's in her 20s and is a real character – a strong personality and a bit of a rebel. She left home because she wanted to be independent and was willing to accept the responsibilities of being independent. She's very animal-oriented and has a cat and lots of stuffed animals. When I went to see her and we went out for a walk, she stopped regularly to put her arms round the dog and praise it. She'd never seen anyone do it, it just came naturally, but the dog loved it. When we got back she took the harness off and immediately picked up the cat.

All she does is three routes – to the park, to the shops and one other. Fortunately she can cope with all the crossings because the roads are either cul-de-sacs or dead-ends that she crosses by going all the way to the bottom, crossing and coming all the way back up again. She realises her limitations and has a very warm relationship with the dog. Nevertheless, there are real problems. If the circumstances of her walks changed, if a cul-de-sac became a through road, she wouldn't be able to cope. If someone asks her if she needs help she can't hear.

So, in very special circumstances, we can achieve a degree of success with some deaf-blind people. It's no more than that.

Characters Remembered

Alan Brooks, senior training manager at the Wokingham centre, recalled in 1988 a few of the guide dog owners he had known.

I remember a Yorkshire man. He used to get up in the morning very early to travel 30 odd miles to work by train. On this occasion it had been snowing heavily all night. The Council had already been out and had dug some paths, for which he was quite thankful, but, as he pointed out, his dog wasn't daft. The path they dug was about a foot wide, so the dog walked in the path and he walked in the snow piled up at the side. So he was going through snow that was even deeper than normal.

He didn't mind that too much because he was a fairly resilient character, and what happened was that where the snow was packed deep he walked up much higher than the dog and then he dropped down again. This carried on for some distance to the station and eventually he walked along and the dog was about a foot or eighteen inches below him. Suddenly he stepped off into mid-air, came down with one hell of a crash and bit his tongue.

The stupid beggars on the Council had piled all the snow up by a bench and he had walked along the bench and off the end of it. He also told me that he used to get on the train to travel home and, totally contrary to the rules, he used to lie on the seat. He had an Alsatian at the time, and he used to get that to lie on the other seat. He would get on early, find an empty compartment to sit in, take his teeth out, pull a few faces and lie on the seat with the dog on the other seat. People used to avoid sitting in his compartment and he used to get it to himself and sleep all the way back home. It worked very well until he ended up one day in Carlisle. He had over-slept and gone past his station, and there wasn't another train back until 8 o'clock the following morning.

However, the station staff managed to find a freight train going back. The freight train was full of cattle and he ended up, both him and the dog, sitting on the coal behind the steam engine. He still didn't get home till 2 o'clock in the morning!

There was one young man who was at university and he taught his dog to find locations by using a name. While he was at university he had various campuses to visit throughout Manchester and he had a name for each room he went to, one of which was the Madhouse, which I suppose was appropriate at university. And he estimates that the dog could learn 40 different locations.

He would recognise 40 different names, 40 different words and when one of those words was spoken the dog would be able to take his owner to that location.

One guide dog owner I knew had a very long tube journey and he regularly went to sleep on the train. He kept some biscuits in his pocket and when he first got the dog he would give it a biscuit at the station before he got off. He taught the dog to bark for the biscuit so he was able to have a sleep, and at the station before he got off, the dog would bark for his biscuit. The man would wake up, give the dog its biscuit and get off at the next stop.

• •

✻ ✻ ✻

I don't know about the best guide dog owner or the best guide dog. I know whom I would feel proudest of. I trained one woman who had been brought up in institutions all her life. At one time she was identified as mentally subnormal but that wasn't the case, it was because she was institutionalised and had never had the stimulation. At the age of 52 she married, still living in institutions. She managed to get her own home two years later, lived with the husband for two years until he died and a year later she decided she wanted a guide dog. So in her mid/late 50s she came for a guide dog.

She was a very difficult lady to train because her education had been very limited, her understanding, her perception of the world around her was limited because she had always lived in sheltered accommodation, always been looked after and had never had any responsibility in her life until she married.

I managed to train her, and she went away from here thrilled to bits, totally in love with the dog. It was one of the few occasions she had had any responsibility in her life and she fulfilled the responsibility. All she did was get out, get her own pension, get her own shopping and live her own little life and visit one or two friends for coffee. But that was a more fulfilled life than she had ever had before.

And that for me was very satisfying.

✻ ✻ ✻

We have a guide dog owner in Kent who got his first dog at the age of 85. I asked him what he did for a living before he retired and he told me he was a transport manager for the Co-op for 55 years. So I said you must have really enjoyed it to stick it for so long and he said, "I did, but it was never quite the same after they brought motor cars in".

He is still alive. He is now in his 91st year, still with his dog. His life consists of getting up in the morning, letting his dog in the garden, getting himself some breakfast and listening to the radio. The dog comes in about 11 o'clock, he harnesses it up, walks a mile to his daughter and his daughter cooks him lunch. In the afternoon she takes the dog to the park while he has a snooze. Later on in the afternoon, harness on again and back home, feeds his dog, listens to his radio, has his tea. In the evening, harness on again and round to the British Legion for a couple of pints with his pals and back home.

Now that's his lifestyle, every day. At 91 he is still able to walk that mile to his daughter, the mile home and then down to the British Legion and back independently.

[Dan Pearce, who was remembered here, died in 1990]

Superdog?
A light-hearted story from the Scottish Sunday Post *to end this anthology. One day, perhaps!*
Jimmy is blind, but he gets around very well with his dog, Sadie.

As the two of them waited at the bus stop the other morning, Jimmy overheard a young boy's voice behind him asking the time.

Jimmy was stooping to check that Sadie's harness was correctly fastened.

Touching his fingers to his braille wrist-watch, he said over his shoulder, "It's twenty to nine."

"Gosh," came the youngster's awed whisper to his chum. "That dog told him the time!"